THE GEORGIA BULLDOGS PLAYBOOK

Inside the Huddle for the
Greatest Plays in Bulldogs History

Patrick Garbin

TRIUMPH
BOOKS

This book is available in quantity at special discounts for your group or organization. For further information, contact:

Triumph Books LLC
814 North Franklin Street
Chicago, Illinois 60610
(312) 337-0747
www.triumphbooks.com

Printed in U.S.A.
ISBN: 978-1-62937-122-1
Design by Patricia Frey

CONTENTS

Foreword *by Charley Trippi*
v

Acknowledgments
vii

Introduction
ix

When It Mattered Most
1

On the Offensive
47

The Best Offense Is a Good Defense
159

Special Consideration
201

Heartbreakers
239

Sources
259

FOREWORD

During my 1941 freshman season, Coach Butts was determined that Georgia must develop a new tradition in football. In those days the practice field was located adjacent to Sanford Stadium. If the team's practice did not suit Coach Butts, he would move us to the stadium to practice at night under the lights. Sometimes we would not eat dinner until 8:00! The practices were long, hard, and very physical. Coach Butts was a tough taskmaster, demanding excellence at all times. If you gave 100 percent, he wanted an additional 10 percent. As it turned out, all of our hard work eventually paid off.

Against Auburn that season, the score was tied 0–0, and there was time for Georgia to run only one more play. Usually freshmen sat in the stands, but for that game I was on the bench in my street clothes. Frank [Sinkwich] was a tremendous runner from tackle to tackle, but he was also an excellent passer. We also envied another teammate of ours, Lamar "Racehorse" Davis, because he had so much speed. Whenever Frank wanted to throw a long pass, he usually looked for Davis because he could get open and no one would be able to catch him. When the two connected on a long pass in the game's final play to beat Auburn, it was the beginning of a new tradition.

It is amazing how sometimes one play can change the complexion of an entire game. I frequently noticed this during my years playing football and many times since. Often, a single play also determines who wins or loses the game—as was the case against Auburn my freshman year.

In my 19 years of playing organized football, I was fortunate to be a part of several memorable and great plays.

My long punt return against Tulsa in the 1946 Oil Bowl was somewhat unique because of the method I used to score. In a close game, I remember catching the punt and starting to my left, but I was trapped. So, I reversed my field toward the right, and I was in the same unfortunate situation. Reversing for a second time toward the left, I finally began to get some blocking and started to head down the sideline. Suddenly, two Tulsa men converged on me, and the only thing I could do was lower my shoulder. When I did, the three of us collided, but fortunately the two Tulsa defenders fell off me, and I went into the end zone for a touchdown.

In another close game against Alabama the following season, we decided to quick-kick near our own goal line. Alabama's Charley Compton came through and blocked my kick. We both chased the football, and I was able to recover it close to our end zone. With many yards to go, I had no alternative but to punt, and I was able to kick the football out of dangerous territory and keep the Crimson Tide from having a short field. My recovery and long punt, as was the case with my return in the Oil Bowl, probably changed the outcomes of those games, resulting in Bulldogs victories.

I have always been very proud to be associated with Georgia football, even during the intermittent tough times the program has experienced in the past. I am extremely proud now, as the Bulldogs have a tremendous program. And speaking of great plays and victories, Georgia has definitely had its share since Coach Richt's arrival.

When I played for Georgia, half of our team was from Ohio or Pennsylvania. Now, Georgia seems to be able to recruit from anywhere it desires. Recruiting is the key to winning football. I have always said that you don't win games in the fall; you win them in the winter or spring when you recruit your players. Most people do not realize that.

What a privilege it must be today to be a part of the University of Georgia's extraordinary football program and to use its first-class facilities. And what a thrill it must be to run out and play in front of more than 92,000 people at Sanford Stadium in Athens, Georgia. That's more spectators than were in attendance at my first bowl game, and we played in the Rose Bowl in Pasadena, California!

—Charley Trippi

ACKNOWLEDGMENTS

This book would not have been possible without the support and assistance of several individuals. I have many fond memories of my parents and I spending precious time with one another, including at my first Georgia football game—a 44–0 win over Tennessee in the season opener of 1981. I want to thank them for, among many other things, their love, inspiration, and encouragement, and for introducing Georgia Bulldogs football to me.

I feel extremely fortunate that Triumph Books took a chance on an unknown author when they asked me to write *"Then Vince Said to Herschel..."* nearly a decade ago. The publishing of my first book had a major impact on my life in many ways, including what has led to me authoring nine books, including seven on Georgia football. I have Triumph Books to thank for making it possible for me to become an author on a subject that has been a passion of mine since I was a child. For this book specifically, I want to thank Triumph's managing editor, Adam Motin, for reaching out to me, working with me, and for his patience.

Although countless photographs exist depicting past and present Georgia football players, coaches, etc., few are readily available related to the greatest plays in Georgia's history. I want to thank the number of sports information departments for contributing photos to this project.

Additionally, the Hargrett Rare Book and Manuscript Library at the University of Georgia was more than generous in helping me find and obtain scarce and seldom-seen photographs. In particular, I want to express my gratitude to photographer Wingate Downs. Fortunately for me, Wingate photographed Georgia games for nearly 20 years and was able to contribute a number of photos to this book. Wingate is regarded as one of the best, if not the best, photographer in Athens, Georgia, and was more than a pleasure to work with.

A special thanks goes to Charley Trippi for writing the foreword to this book. He is not only one of the greatest Bulldogs to ever play football but one of the most premier players to grace any gridiron. It was truly wonderful to spend time with Charley again, and I appreciate his willingness to contribute to this book.

First and foremost, I am forever grateful for my wife, Elizabeth, and our children, Trip and Rebecca. During the many days when I have been absent from our household while researching and writing, my wife has been my principal supporter. Elizabeth, thank you for allowing me to realize my dream and for giving me the two greatest gifts I have ever received.

INTRODUCTION

For nearly 125 years, University of Georgia football has been synonymous with stellar accomplishments surpassed by only a handful of other college programs. Of all FBS teams, Georgia ranks amongst the top dozen all time in victories, bowl appearances, and bowl victories. In addition, five Bulldog teams have been selected national champions by at least one recognized poll. During the most recent seasons, the reputation of the Georgia football program has been somewhat enhanced as the Bulldogs have received a bowl invitation 18 consecutive seasons, achieving a 13–5 bowl record, and nine out of their last 13 teams have won 10 or more games heading into 2015.

Much of the Bulldogs' recent success can be attributed to the arrival of head coach Mark Richt in 2001. For more than a decade prior to the Richt regime, Georgia was considered a second-rate team in the Southeastern Conference. During the head coach's tenure, Richt's teams have altered this perception; the Bulldogs are now one of the most highly regarded teams not only in the conference but in all of college football. Richt now rightly belongs to a group of outstanding Georgia coaches who experienced similar successes, namely, Alex Cunningham, Harry Mehre, Wally Butts, and, of course, Vince Dooley.

These coaching icons have coached some of the most outstanding players in all of college football. Georgia greats who left indelible marks on the program include Bob McWhorter, Vernon "Catfish" Smith, Frank Sinkwich, Charley Trippi, Fran Tarkenton, Bill Stanfill, Jake Scott, Herschel Walker, Terry Hoage, Eric Zeier, David Greene, David Pollack, Todd Gurley, and Nick Chubb, to name only a few. These players and many others have been involved in a countless number of remarkable plays since the program's beginning in 1892. Many of the greatest of these plays are presented in the following pages of this book.

The most important, memorable, or amazing plays in Georgia football history are grouped by category and recounted. Each play is intricately detailed while the game in which it occurred is also summarized. Also included is an explanation as to why the play is so important or memorable in Bulldogs football lore. Besides the main text, each chapter contains a variety of additional material. There are profiles of players and coaches involved in the plays and quotes from individuals who participated in or observed the plays as they unfolded. As an added feature, some plays are diagrammed, presented with the Xs and Os.

More often than not, plays selected were those that were both extraordinary and aided in winning games and/or championships in the contest's final minutes. Remarkable plays that achieved team or player milestones and those that transpired in critical situations having implications for winning or losing games were also considered as my evaluative rationale. Also, the decision was made to consider trick plays, those plays fans may not easily recall (i.e., special teams and defensive plays), and plays executed by opposing teams that were defined as "heartbreakers" because, after all, they also help to make up the history of Georgia football. Understandably, it was a most challenging task to measure these rather loose criteria. Hence, it must be acknowledged that to a considerable extent, the play selection is the end result of an extremely subjective and somewhat arbitrary evaluative process.

Notably, in researching and writing this book, I was reminded of all the great Georgia football plays I have witnessed since I began attending Bulldogs games in the early 1980s. As an example, I will never forget Kevin Butler's 60-yard field goal that defeated Clemson in 1984. After Butler's kick went through the uprights, I remember a drink in a cupful of ice being thrown from the upper deck onto me, my family, and others in the section where we were sitting. But no one really cared. Georgia had just defeated the No. 2–ranked team in the country on a miraculous field goal. As I looked up toward the seats to see where the dropped drink came from, an elderly man sitting near me commented the drink smelled like it had something in it besides Coca-Cola. Sanford Stadium appeared to me, at nine years of age, to literally swing and sway and nearly collapse in excitement. I knew then what Larry Munson meant when he said "the girders are bending now," following an unforgettable Georgia play against Florida in the Gator Bowl that occurred nearly a decade prior. Butler's field goal was the first great Bulldogs play that brought me to tears of euphoria, but not the last.

It is my hope that many readers of this book will relive and re-experience some of the plays described as I did during my research. If *The Georgia Bulldogs Playbook* is able to realize this goal, its author will consider it a success.

WHEN IT MATTERED MOST

THE DOGS BROKE IT UP!

Jeff Sanchez and Ronnie Harris break up Auburn's pass in end zone as Georgia wins third consecutive SEC title

The undefeated Bulldogs entered their game at Auburn in 1982 having just been ranked No. 1 in both major polls only a few days before. The conference championship and a possible national title were at stake for Georgia, whereas a win by the Tigers could propel them to a first-place tie with the 'Dogs in the SEC.

Auburn had one of the most extraordinary running games in college football. Quarterback Randy Campbell, fullback Ron O'Neal, and tailbacks Lionel James and Bo Jackson formed the Tigers' wishbone formation—an offense not normally associated with passing. Despite running the wishbone, however, Auburn's passing attack could be dangerous and was actually much more prolific than Georgia's.

Down 19–14 with 49 seconds remaining in the game, Auburn was on Georgia's 21-yard line but faced a fourth down and 17 for a first down. Campbell, who had some success throwing against an outstanding Georgia secondary, dropped back to throw. He floated a lofty pass in

Auburn's fourth-down pass attempt intended for Mike Edwards (No. 89) is broken up in the end zone by Georgia's Jeff Sanchez (center) and Ronnie Harris (No. 27), clinching a 19–14 Bulldogs victory. *Photo courtesy of Wingate Downs.*

the end zone for split end Mike Edwards. Georgia's safety Jeff Sanchez, cornerback Ronnie Harris, and Edwards all jumped for the ball, but none of them came down with it. The football dropped harmlessly to the turf, and the Bulldogs, taking over on downs, were only 42 seconds away from their third consecutive conference title.

Early in the fourth quarter, with the Tigers trailing by six points, the 5'7", 165-pound James scored on an 87-yard run—at the time, the second-longest rushing or passing play in Auburn history. Losing 14–13, Georgia began its possession from its 20-yard line. Thirteen plays and 80 yards later, Herschel Walker scored on a three-yard run, and the Bulldogs regained the lead. On the drive, Walker rushed for 37 yards on eight carries, and quarterback John Lastinger completed

Vince Dooley receives a victory ride at Auburn, having won his sixth SEC championship (and third in a row) in 19 seasons as Georgia's head coach. *Photo courtesy of Wingate Downs.*

a key third-down-and-six pass to Herman Archie for 17 yards; Georgia completed only three passes for the entire game for 26 yards. Walker finished the contest with 177 rushing yards on 31 carries and two touchdowns en route to eventually capturing the Heisman Trophy.

With a little less than nine minutes left in the game, Auburn began a drive from its own 20-yard line and soon reached Bulldogs territory; a James run carried the ball to Georgia's 14-yard line with 3:04 remaining. A penalty on Auburn moved the ball back five yards, and Georgia's Tony Flack followed by tackling Jackson two yards behind the line of scrimmage. From the 21-yard line, Georgia defensive end Dale Carver made one of the most significant plays of the year for the Bulldogs by sacking Campbell for a nine-yard loss with a little more than a minute

RONNIE HARRIS

Like Jeff Sanchez, Ronnie Harris also attended a California junior college, came to Georgia, and was instantly starting in the Bulldogs' defensive backfield. Harris, from San Diego, earned recognition in his second game at Georgia by intercepting two passes against a team from his home state, the California Golden Bears. From his left cornerback position, Harris led the Bulldogs in '81 with four interceptions, not including the two he corralled against Pittsburgh's Dan Marino in the Sugar Bowl. Harris' two interceptions against the Panthers are tied for a school record for most interceptions in a bowl game.

As a senior in '82, Harris' late interception of Brigham Young University's Steve Young sealed a three-point Georgia victory. Three games later, he would pick off two passes against Ole Miss. Harris finished his final season as a Bulldog with four interceptions and was chosen to play in the 1983 Japan Bowl, a college all-star game.

Following college, Harris made the roster of the 1985 Chicago Blitz of the United States Football League. He currently is a social studies teacher and head coach at Oglethorpe County Middle School, located in Lexington, Georgia.

THE BREAKUP

As four receivers ran toward Georgia's end zone, Auburn quarterback Randy Campbell dropped back to pass. As a Bulldogs defender rushed up the middle and another blitzed from his left, Campbell was forced to throw earlier than desired. He barely got off a high, wobbly pass from his 29. The desperation heave descended left of intended receiver Mike Edwards and fell incomplete between Georgia's Jeff Sanchez and Ronnie Harris.

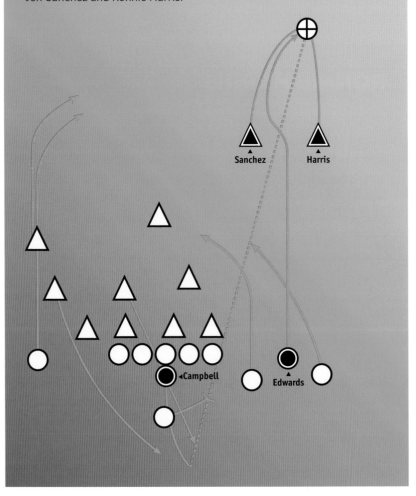

left on the clock. On third and 26, from the 30-yard line, Campbell completed a nine-yard pass to tight end Ed West.

On Campbell's fourth-down pass into the end zone, Edwards, the intended target, later claimed all he saw were two Bulldogs defenders leaping in front of him. Edwards had been lined up on the outside with Georgia's Harris while Sanchez was positioned on the inside with a different receiver. As Campbell threw toward Edwards, Sanchez abandoned his man and went for the ball. Both Sanchez and Harris leapt for the ball in front of Edwards and broke up the potential winning pass.

From its 21-yard line, Georgia ran out the remaining seconds on the clock and seized a 19–14 victory. Soon afterward, coach Vince Dooley was carried off Auburn's field on the shoulders of his players, celebrating his 150th career victory and his sixth Southeastern Conference championship.

Game Details

Georgia 19 • Auburn 14

Date: November 13, 1982

Site: Jordan-Hare Stadium

Attendance: 74,800

Records: Georgia 9–0; Auburn 7–2

Rankings: Georgia: No. 1 (AP)/ No. 1 (UPI)

Series: Georgia 40–38–7 (Georgia two-game winning streak)

> [The defense] had our backs to the wall, and we had to stand up and fight.
>
> **—Ronnie Harris, Georgia cornerback**

"ONSIDE KICK" ULTIMATELY WINS CHAMPIONSHIP

Misplayed kickoff in 1981 Sugar Bowl is the difference in a win over Notre Dame

At the conclusion of the 1980 regular season, perhaps never before in college football had there been so many questions regarding which team deserved to be ranked No. 1. Georgia ended its regular season ranked first in both major polls and with a perfect record, the only major college football team to finish unscathed. Nevertheless, there was some question as to whether or not Georgia was entitled to play for the national championship. The Bulldogs were receiving little respect from those in the media or their opponent in the upcoming Sugar Bowl, the University of Notre Dame. Georgia's schedule was perceived as having been weak, and the Bulldogs were one-point underdogs to the Fighting Irish. Many felt Georgia would need the luck of the Irish to defeat Notre Dame.

At the bottom of this pile, with the football, is Georgia's Bob Kelly. His recovery of a misplayed kickoff against Notre Dame in the 1981 Sugar Bowl was the key play in winning the game and ensuring the Bulldogs' eventual capturing of the national title. *Photo courtesy of Wingate Downs.*

Georgia's Rex Robinson kicked off late in the opening quarter of a 3–3 tie game. Robinson's high kick drifted down around the 5-yard line. Notre Dame's Jim Stone and Ty Barber did not field the ball, which bounced between the two return men. Stone, realizing their mistake, attempted to recover the bouncing and free ball. As Georgia's Steve Kelly blocked Stone away from the play, his brother Bob Kelly recovered the ball on Notre Dame's 1-yard line. After the change of possession, Georgia's Herschel Walker dove into the end zone for a touchdown two plays later. The Bulldogs had capitalized on a critical Notre Dame

THE KELLY BROTHERS

Bob and Steve Kelly were both stars at Benedictine High School in Savannah, Georgia. Bob, two years older, played for Furman University in 1976 but transferred to Georgia after one year. In 1978 he was the Bulldogs' starting safety as only a sophomore and recorded 57 tackles and one interception on Georgia's nine-win squad. However, in his final two years, Bob was relegated to playing reserve defensive back and on special teams.

Georgia's third tailback as a true freshman in 1978, Steve finished his sophomore season as the Bulldogs' starting tailback. In 1979 he averaged 5.6 yards per carry with 459 yards rushing, including 117 yards

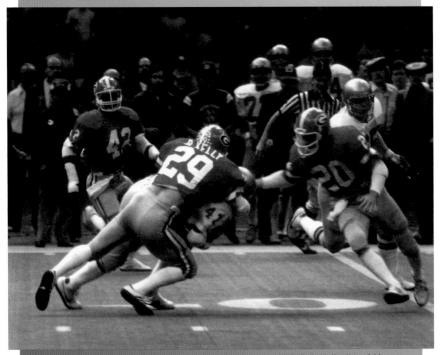

After starting for Georgia at safety as a sophomore in 1978, Bob Kelly (No. 29) played only a reserve role in his final two seasons. Nevertheless, in his final game as a Bulldog, Kelly made one of the greatest plays in school history. *Photo courtesy of Wingate Downs.*

on 13 attempts in a 16–3 win over Georgia Tech in the season finale. However, as the 1980 season began, Georgia had a number of quality players at the tailback position, including freshman Herschel Walker. Steve was moved to cornerback and played sparingly as a third-string junior.

How deserving it was when Catholic brothers Bob and Steve, both demoted during their times at Georgia, teamed up to make a spectacular play against Notre Dame with the national championship at stake. Bob, whom Vince Dooley has called the ultimate team player, commented following Georgia's win over the Fighting Irish that the Bulldogs in 1980, as a team, never overpowered anyone, "but we always just seem to be there to make the play."

Steve with the block on the kick returner and Bob with the recovered kick, the Kelly brothers certainly were there to make an unforgettable play in the 1981 Sugar Bowl.

mistake by recovering, in essence, a 59-yard onside kick, which led to a 10–3 lead.

On the first possession of the game, the Fighting Irish passed their way down the field to a field goal by Harry Oliver. Georgia's initial offensive drive resulted in Walker separating his shoulder on the second play and the Bulldogs losing yardage and being forced to punt. Notre Dame came right down the field again and set up for another Oliver field goal. Seldom-used freshman Terry Hoage blocked Oliver's kick, and instead of trailing 6–0, the Bulldogs had the ball in Fighting Irish territory down by only three points.

Georgia reached Notre Dame's 18-yard line, but an 11-yard sack of quarterback Buck Belue forced the Bulldogs to attempt a field goal on fourth down. Robinson's 46-yard field goal was successful, and the game was tied.

The ensuing kickoff has been called "one of the strangest plays in the history of college football." For Georgia, however, it was one of the greatest. Fortunately, Stone and Barber were fielding the kick near a loud and raucous Bulldogs crowd. Stone, the "call-man," called for Barber to field Robinson's kick, but Barber could not hear him over the crowd noise. The two had also misplayed the bowl's opening kickoff because of the noise, although Stone was able to recover and down the kick in the end zone. This time, however, there was no recovery for Notre Dame as the older Kelly brother gladly accepted the Irish's gift just outside the goal line.

After the recovered kick, Belue was stopped for no gain, but Walker, fully recovered from his injury, scored on second down and Georgia took a lead it would never relinquish.

The Hoage-blocked field goal and the recovered kickoff were just two of several mistakes made by Notre Dame in losing the Sugar Bowl. On the Fighting Irish's first possession of the second quarter, they fumbled deep in their own territory, and Georgia recovered on the

Game Details

Georgia 17 • Notre Dame 10

Date: January 1, 1981

Site: Superdome

Attendance: 77,895

Records: Georgia 11–0; Notre Dame 9–1–1

Rankings: Georgia: No. 1 (AP)/ No. 1 (UPI); Notre Dame: No. 7 (AP)/ No. 8 (UPI)

Series: First meeting

> Ty just didn't hear me.... It was the crowd; it was pretty loud.
>
> **—Jim Stone, Notre Dame kick returner**

22-yard line. Three plays later, Walker scored again, and the Bulldogs led 17–3.

In Georgia's 17–10 win over Notre Dame, the Bulldogs were outperformed in every statistical facet of the game, except the number of miscues. The Fighting Irish's consequential errors included three interceptions, one fumble, a blocked field goal, and two missed field goals. However, none was bigger than the Bulldogs' first-quarter "onside kick"—the difference in the University of Georgia capturing its first undisputed national title in any sport.

Two plays after Kelly's recovery, freshman Herschel Walker dives into the end zone for the Sugar Bowl's first touchdown. Slightly more than two minutes later, Walker would score again, and Georgia would eventually win 17–10. *Photo courtesy of AP Images.*

FUMBLE HOOKS 'HORNS

Texas fumbles punt to Bulldogs and loses '84 Cotton Bowl and national title

Georgia's loss to Auburn in 1983 broke the Bulldogs' consecutive streak of three Southeastern Conference titles and Sugar Bowl appearances. Georgia's consolation was a trip to the Cotton Bowl to face second-ranked Texas, the Southwest Conference champion. The Longhorns were undefeated, practically playing a home game in Dallas, and were the favorite by more than a touchdown. In addition, Texas' defense was considered perhaps the most dominant ever in college football. Texas was also aware that a defeat of Georgia, coupled with a win by Miami of Florida over top-ranked Nebraska on the same day would result in the Longhorns being named national champions. Some of the Texas players had even admitted that the Nebraska-Miami matchup later that night in the Orange Bowl was in the back of their minds leading up to their game against Georgia.

Trailing by six points and facing fourth down at their 34-yard line with 4:32 remaining in the game, the Bulldogs elected to punt to Texas,

Three plays after Gary Moss' game-changing fumble recovery in the 1984 Cotton Bowl, quarterback John Lastinger scores the winning touchdown on a 17-yard run. *Photo courtesy of AP Images.*

hoping their defense could hold the Longhorns for one more possession. Punter Chip Andrews hung a high, short punt over Texas' 30-yard line. Longhorn defensive back Craig Curry tried an over-the-shoulder catch of the ball just as Georgia's Melvin Simmons shouted, "Miss it, miss it!"

Curry obliged and dropped the punt. Jitter Fields, Texas' regular punt returner, could not recover his teammate's fumble as the ball squirted through his arms during a mad scramble. Special teams player Gary Moss of Georgia recovered Curry's blunder on the Longhorns' 23-yard line and gave the Bulldogs a rare scoring opportunity.

Normally accurate kickers Jeff Ward of Texas and Georgia's Kevin Butler had combined to make only four of eight field goals during the first 55-plus minutes of play as the Longhorns led 9–3. The Bulldogs would need some sort of break for a Cotton Bowl victory as their offense had struggled mightily against Texas' vaunted defense.

Game Details

Georgia 10 • Texas 9

Date: January 2, 1984

Site: Cotton Bowl

Attendance: 67,891

Records: Georgia 9-1-1; Texas 11-0

Rankings: Georgia: No. 7 (AP)/ No. 7 (UPI); Texas: No. 2 (AP)/ No. 2 (UPI)

Series: Texas 3-0 (Texas three-game winning streak)

> I have no excuses [for fumbling]. I don't know why I did it.
>
> **—Craig Curry, Texas defensive back**

Seniors John Lastinger (No. 12), Terry Hoage (No. 14), and Guy McIntyre (No. 74) crowd around the winners' trophy with Coach Vince Dooley following Georgia's 10–9 upset victory over Texas in the Cotton Bowl. *Photo courtesy of AP Images.*

As Georgia lined up to punt, Texas head coach Fred Akers sensed a Bulldogs fake and left his first-team defense on the field, inserting only Fields. Akers also instructed Curry, who had never fielded a punt as a Longhorn, to not attempt to catch the ball if Georgia did indeed punt. Coach Vince Dooley said following the game a fake punt never entered his mind; there was too much time left on the clock.

For whatever reason, Curry did not abide by his coach's demands, and his first attempt at returning a punt ended in tragedy with Moss' recovery. Georgia gained six yards in two plays to Texas' 17-yard line. On third down and four, quarterback John Lastinger forced Curry into another mistake. Lastinger ran an option to his right, and Curry decided to take the pitchman, Tron Jackson. Instead, Lastinger turned upfield and dashed into the end zone for the game-winning touchdown with 3:22 remaining. Butler's extra point broke the tie and gave the Bulldogs a 10–9 lead.

On the ensuing possession, Texas ran three plays and was forced to punt. Georgia got the ball back and ran the clock out, converting a fourth and one on the Longhorns' 36-yard line in the process.

A sobbing Curry left the Texas dressing room only 45 minutes following the game, avoiding the media altogether. He had made two deciding mistakes; his first, the muffed punt, was the turning point in Georgia's improbable victory.

GARY MOSS

Gary Moss, who began his Georgia career as a reserve cornerback, had moved to tailback by the end of the '83 season. Ironically, the converted rusher made one of the greatest special teams plays in Georgia football history and, later, was a standout defensive back in his final two seasons.

As a sophomore in 1983, Moss intercepted one pass (before moving to tailback) and led the team in kickoff returns with a 23.0 average on eight returns. Besides his unforgettable fumble recovery in the '84 Cotton Bowl, Moss also made a tackle on special teams and returned three punts for 57 yards.

After sitting out the 1984 season, Moss became one of Georgia's most highly regarded defensive backs of the 1980s. He led the Bulldogs in interceptions in 1985 and 1986, finishing his career with 10, which still ranks among the school's career leaders. Moss also broke up a combined 20 passes in his junior and senior seasons.

After college Moss played for the Atlanta Falcons' scab team during the 1987 NFL strike. As he had done while at Georgia, Moss returned punts and kickoffs and also intercepted a pass in three games.

En route to a 10–1–1 record and a No. 4 national ranking, the 1983 Georgia Bulldogs, led by the program's most accomplished class of seniors in history, often had to find ways to win. It was no different in the '84 Cotton Bowl. The overconfident Longhorns, on the other hand, found a way to lose as they looked forward to a game other than their own and a national title that never materialized.

CHIP ANDREWS

Chip Andrews was Georgia's starting punter in 1983 and 1984 after transferring from the University of Tennessee at Chattanooga in '80, redshirting in '81, and playing junior varsity in 1982. During his collegiate career, Andrews had a reputation for producing lofty and lengthy punts. Of the 25 Bulldogs who have punted at least 50 times since the mid-1940s, Andrews' 43.2 average on 109 career punts ranks second to Drew Butler's 45.4.

However, it was a short punt by Andrews that led to Georgia's celebrated fumble recovery against Texas. The shortened punt surprised Texas' Fred Akers, who later admitted he thought Andrews would kick it farther. A longer punt likely would have been fielded by Jitter Fields and not Craig Curry and in turn, probably not muffed. Andrews averaged 41.2 yards on nine punts in the Cotton Bowl.

Andrews was drafted by the United States Football League's Jacksonville Bulls in the 1985 territorial draft but never saw any playing time.

PHENOMENAL CATCH FORCES OVERTIME

Corey Allen's touchdown reception ties the Tigers in '96, initiating the first of four overtimes

In the 100th edition of the Deep South's oldest rivalry, Georgia slumped into 20th-ranked Auburn University's Jordan-Hare Stadium with perhaps its worst team in 35 years. The Bulldogs seniors had a losing 20–21–1 overall record since 1993, including a deplorable 0–12–1 mark versus rivals Florida, Tennessee, Alabama, and Auburn. Quarterback Mike Bobo and running back Robert Edwards, preseason all-conference contenders, were benched following their lackluster performances in a 47–7 loss to Florida two weeks prior to the Auburn meeting. The junior Bobo, who had promising freshman and sophomore campaigns, was completing fewer than half his passes for the season and led the Southeastern Conference in interceptions (15), including nine in the previous four games, compared to a single touchdown pass. Starting in his place was Brian Smith, a fifth-year senior

On the last regulation play against Auburn in 1996, quarterback Mike Bobo threw a 30-yard touchdown pass to Corey Allen, forcing the first overtime contest in SEC history.
Photo courtesy of AP Images.

JIM DONNAN

What was called the "Donnan of a New Era" when Jim Donnan arrived at Georgia in 1996 from a successful six-season stint at Marshall University soon turned to despair when the Bulldogs lost their season opener to Southern Mississippi—10½-point underdogs. Donnan would soon turn the program around, recording a 10-2 mark in 1997—twice as many victories as his first campaign. Nine- and eight-win seasons followed for three years, but it was not quite good enough for Georgia administrators. Donnan's contract was terminated following the 2000 season and five years at the helm. Although he had been successful in elevating the football program to a higher level than his predecessor Ray Goff, the Bulldogs were still regarded as a second-rate program in the

The 56-49 win over Auburn in four overtimes was one of Coach Jim Donnan's biggest victories during his five-year tenure at Georgia. Pictured is Donnan coaching his final game as a Bulldog—a 37-14 win over Virginia in the 2000 Oahu Bowl. *Photo courtesy of Getty Images.*

who had thrown for minus-one yard for the year on two of five passing. The Bulldogs had not defeated a ranked opponent in nearly four years, and it appeared likely they would not do so in the imminent future.

Toward the end of the game, Georgia was the benefactor of a gratuitous act by Auburn, but it should have been another defeat and the final horn of the centennial meeting. Instead, the Bulldogs had the ball on the Tigers' 30-yard line with one second remaining and trailing 28–21. Bobo, who had come off the bench late in the first half, took the snap and rolled to his right as time expired. He lofted a strike to a leaping Corey Allen, who made the catch just in front of the goal line. While in the air, Allen twisted and lunged over the front right corner of the end zone for an improbable touchdown.

Georgia was losing 28–7 late in the second quarter when quarterback Smith was replaced by Bobo. The former starter aroused a stagnant offense, completing 21 of 37 passes in the game for 360 yards, two touchdowns, and no interceptions. Despite playing with a minor concussion, receiver Hines Ward totaled 251 all-purpose yards, including 67 on a scoring pass from Bobo early in the final quarter to reduce the Bulldogs' deficit to seven points.

Down 28–21, Georgia got the ball on its own 18-yard line with no timeouts and only 1:07 left in the game. Bobo, who completed only one of six passes in the Bulldogs' previous possession, threw incomplete on first down. On the next play, he connected with Ward for a 15-yard gain. Five consecutive completions later, Bobo had driven Georgia to Auburn's 21-yard line. With fewer than 10 seconds remaining, Bobo was sacked for a nine-yard loss by Marcus Washington, and the game clock was about to expire. Fortunately for Georgia, Auburn sophomore Charles Dorsey, thinking the game was over, grabbed the football after Bobo had been sacked. The officials stopped the clock with six seconds left to spot the ball. This allowed Bobo to spike the football on the next play, stopping the clock with one final second remaining.

During Allen's leaping and twisting touchdown, the junior's first points at Georgia, a flag was thrown by an official. After the miraculous score, Allen inquired about the penalty and was told he had been interfered with by Auburn's Jayson Bray. Georgia's touchdown pass stood, and the Bulldogs were only an extra point away from sending the game into the conference's first overtime period (the NCAA adopted overtime for Division I-A football at the start of the 1995 bowl season).

Hap Hines' successful point-after kick forced the beginning of what would eventually be four overtime periods. On the fourth and final extra

Game Details

Georgia 56 • Auburn 49 (four overtimes)

Date: November 16, 1996

Site: Jordan-Hare Stadium

Attendance: 85,214

Records: Georgia 3–5; Auburn 7–2

Rankings: Auburn: No. 20 (AP)/ No. 21 (CNN)

Series: Auburn 47–44–8 (Auburn three-game nonlosing streak)

> When I caught it, I knew it wasn't in [the end zone].... I tried to wiggle and get the ball across.
>
> **—Corey Allen, Georgia wide receiver**

frame, Georgia's Torin Kirtsey rushed for a one-yard touchdown, and Hines' conversion gave the Bulldogs a 56–49 advantage. On Auburn's ensuing possession, quarterback Dameyune Craig was stopped just short of a first down on fourth and three from Georgia's 18-yard line.

After the comeback victory, Georgia's first-year coach Jim Donnan said, "We needed this to step up respectability."

For one of the few times during a substandard, four-year period, the Bulldogs finally earned a measure of respect in defeating a superior opponent.

MIKE BOBO

Mike Bobo's play was certainly encouraging as Eric Zeier's backup in 1994 and before a fractured knee in Georgia's fourth game of 1995 forced Bobo to sit out the rest of his sophomore season. However, Bobo's early success, for whatever reason, did not continue into the following year.

Under a new coach, Bobo suffered, as did the entire team, for the first eight games of 1996. After being benched most of the first half against Auburn, Bobo responded by performing exceptionally well in Georgia's final three games and through the end of his senior season in 1997. In Bobo's final 15 games as the Bulldogs' quarterback, including the '98 Outback Bowl, he remarkably completed 65.1 percent of his passes for 3,934 yards, 26 touchdowns, and just nine interceptions as Georgia won 12 of the 15 games. Bobo's 155.8 passing rating in '97 ranked sixth highest in the nation and remains third in school history.

Bobo served as an administrative assistant and graduate assistant at Georgia in 1998 and 1999. After coaching Jacksonville State's quarterbacks in 2000, Bobo was brought back to Athens by Mark Richt in 2001. He began calling Georgia's offensive plays in the '06 Georgia Tech game and was promoted to offensive coordinator in 2007. He remained with the Bulldogs until taking over as head coach at Colorado State in 2015.

70-X-TAKEOFF SNATCHES EASTERN TITLE

David Greene's fourth-down pass to Michael Johnson upends Auburn and takes SEC East in '02

Entering the 2002 season, Georgia was in the same predicament as South Carolina, Kentucky, and Vanderbilt, having never won an SEC East title since the conference split into divisions in 1992. During the Bulldogs' 10-season absence from the SEC title game, Tennessee made the trip to the championship three times, while Florida did it on seven occasions. However, Georgia won its first eight games of the '02 campaign and was in prime position to take its initial divisional title before a 20–13 loss to Florida put the Bulldogs' quest on hold. After a win over Ole Miss, Georgia needed to defeat Auburn to capture the SEC East. The nationally ranked Tigers were playing at home and would be benefiting from the Bulldogs having lost two of their top three wide receivers: split end Terrence Edwards and flanker Damien Gary. Georgia's injuries would force a little-known

Michael Johnson leaps over Auburn's Horace Willis to catch David Greene's fourth-down pass in 2002. Johnson's scoring reception with 1:25 remaining to play gave the Bulldogs a lead they maintained through the end of the game, clinching their first SEC East title. *Photo courtesy of Getty Images.*

Interestingly, several of David Greene's family members, including his father, attended Auburn University. Prior to his senior year in high school, Greene visited Auburn on a recruiting trip but was largely ignored by assistant coaches. Auburn's disregard would eventually come back to haunt the Tigers.

Greene first made a name for himself in only his fourth game as a redshirt freshman, guiding Georgia on its game-winning drive in an upset over Tennessee on the road. He was eventually chosen Southeastern Conference Freshman of the Year in 2001 and followed as the conference's Offensive Player of the Year as only a sophomore. In

Late in the fourth quarter, David Greene and Coach Mark Richt discuss strategy just prior to Greene's winning touchdown toss against Auburn. *Photo courtesy of AP Images.*

addition to Auburn in 2002, Greene directed two other fourth-quarter comebacks (Clemson and Alabama) as Georgia won 13 games, its first SEC title in 20 years, and was Sugar Bowl champion. Two years later, Greene finished an unprecedented and brilliant collegiate career. When he left, the three-time All-SEC performer held many school records, including a conference-record 11,528 career passing yards. Greene was the winningest Division I-A quarterback in history with a 42-10 career record as a starter and remains one of the greatest quarterbacks ever at Georgia.

Greene spent time with Seattle (2005-2006), Kansas City (2007), New England (2007), and Indianapolis (2008) in the NFL since being a third-round selection in the 2005 draft.

receiver into action and involve him in one of the greatest plays in school history.

The Bulldogs trailed the Tigers 21–17 with only 1:31 remaining in the game. Georgia was on Auburn's 19-yard line but had no timeouts and was confronted by a fourth down and 15; a victory and a divisional title appeared highly doubtful.

With Michael Johnson to his left and Mario Raley and Fred Gibson on the right, quarterback David Greene took the snap from a shotgun formation. After a short drop, he pump-faked a pass toward Gibson, hoping to draw Auburn's free safety to Georgia's talented flanker. Greene suddenly shifted and lofted a pass in the back left corner of the end zone toward Johnson. The 6'3", 215-pound split end turned and leaped over Auburn cornerback Horace Willis. Johnson caught Greene's pass with both hands and pulled it away from the defender, outfighting Willis for the ball. The Bulldogs had scored an inconceivable touchdown by the reserve receiver and had taken their first lead of the game with 1:25 to play.

Georgia was behind, 14–3, at halftime, but the deficit would have been greater were it not for free safety Sean Jones' two interceptions and a fumble recovery in the first half. Late in the third quarter, a

Georgia touchdown cut Auburn's lead to four points. Nevertheless, the Bulldogs' chances at a possible victory seemed to disappear when they lost the ball on downs with 2:33 remaining in the fourth quarter; however, the Tigers, for their sixth consecutive possession, ran three plays and were forced to punt.

Georgia began its final drive on its own 41-yard line. On second down and six from the 45, Greene connected with Gibson for a 41-yard gain with 1:46 left on the clock. From Auburn's 14-yard line, Greene threw three consecutive incomplete passes while the team committed a five-yard false start penalty.

Facing fourth down and long, the play was brought in from the sideline—70-X-Takeoff—and Greene added in the huddle, "Let's go get

MICHAEL JOHNSON

A big, strong, and physical receiver, Michael Johnson did not see playing time as a Bulldog until the season opener of his third season at Georgia. Entering the '02 Auburn game, the junior receiver had made only six career starts and 18 catches in nearly two entire seasons. Injuries to Terrence Edwards and Damien Gary propelled Johnson as the Bulldogs' starting split end and David Greene's primary target against the Tigers. In recording one of the best receiving performances in school history, Johnson caught 13 passes for 141 yards, including his fourth-down touchdown grab. Only minutes prior to his game-winning reception, Johnson had fumbled following a 10-yard gain, halting a Georgia drive in Auburn territory with the Bulldogs trailing 21–17. Three Georgia possessions later, he more than made up for his earlier blunder.

As a senior in 2003, Johnson finished fourth on the team in receiving, catching 27 passes for 361 yards. Despite playing in only three seasons and making 12 career starts, Johnson caught 62 passes for 847 yards. Few catches, however, were as significant as his 19-yarder for a touchdown that toppled the Tigers in 2002 and gave the Bulldogs their first SEC East title.

it." The play was designed for both Johnson and Gibson to run straight into the end zone. Gibson was designated the decoy while Johnson, or the X, would be the primary receiver. Coach Mark Richt said later he felt that of the receivers, Johnson had the better chance of catching a thrown jump ball. Gibson, considered one of the best receivers in the conference, would certainly be covered thoroughly by the Tigers' secondary. Furthermore, Gibson had a cast on the base of his left hand.

As he broke the huddle and lined up opposite Willis, who was a former Bulldogs signee from Mableton, Georgia, Johnson later recalled he did not want to let the Bulldog Nation down. A minute and a half later, the Bulldogs had defeated the Tigers on "the Plains," 24–21. The substitute receiver had accomplished the exact opposite of what he wanted to avoid, securing a title for the Bulldogs and their Nation.

Game Details

Georgia 24 • Auburn 21

Date: November 16, 2002

Site: Jordan-Hare Stadium

Attendance: 86,063

Records: Georgia 9–1; Auburn 7–3

Rankings: Georgia: No. 7 (AP)/ No. 7 (ESPN); Auburn: No. 24 (AP)

Series: Auburn 51–46–8 (Auburn three-game winning streak)

> I wasn't even open, but I had to make the play.
>
> **—Michael Johnson, wide receiver**

TARKENTON TAMES TIGERS

Fran Tarkenton tosses a 13-yard touchdown on fourth down to defeat Auburn and capture SEC title

Perhaps the worst period in Georgia football was during the 1950s. As the decade forged on, the Bulldogs seemingly got worse with each passing season. However, the 1959 campaign was, if you will, a diamond in the rough—a rare successful year amidst 15 seasons of disappointment. The Bulldogs entered their game against Auburn with a surprising 7–1 record and a No. 12 national ranking—team bests in 11 years. On the other hand, the rival Tigers were considered one of the better squads in college football during the latter part of the decade. Since mid-November 1956, eighth-ranked Auburn had a spectacular 29–1–1 record, had won conference and national titles in '57, and needed a win over the Bulldogs in 1959 for a second Southeastern Conference crown.

With only 30 seconds remaining in the game, Georgia had the ball on Auburn's 13-yard line, trailing 13–7. It was fourth down, and the Bulldogs had only one final chance at victory and the conference championship. Quarterback Fran

> Bill Herron came through like a champion on the winning TD pass, and so did Tarkenton.
>
> **—Wally Butts, Georgia head coach**

Injured during the 1959 season, end Bill Herron caught only eight passes all year. However, his fourth-down touchdown reception from Fran Tarkenton to defeat Auburn is one of the greatest pass catches in the history of SEC football. *Photo courtesy of Hargrett Rare Book & Manuscript Library/University of Georgia Libraries.*

BILL HERRON

Bill Herron likely would have had an outstanding career at Georgia, according to coach Wally Butts, but he was injured for most of the two seasons he was a Bulldog. A native of Sanger, California, Herron played at Fresno Junior College and was highly recruited to play major college football. Against Texas in the 1958 season opener, Herron injured his neck, an injury that persisted during his collegiate career.

In his senior season of 1959, Herron caught eight passes for 135 yards and two touchdowns, not including his two receptions for 26 yards against Missouri in the Orange Bowl.

Herron played one season in the Canadian Football League before suffering another injury. He returned to California, where he worked for a finance company for nearly three decades. Today, the retiree lives on a 20-acre ranch.

After his touchdown catch clinched an SEC championship, Bill Herron and the rest of the 1959 Bulldogs earned a trip to the Orange Bowl to face Missouri. Pictured is Herron tackling Missouri's Fred Brossart on a punt return during a 14–0 Georgia win. *Photo courtesy of AP Images.*

Tarkenton took the snap and rolled to his right, decoying the defense and pretending to look to halfback Bobby Towns. Suddenly, Tarkenton turned and sailed a pass across the field to his left to end Bill Herron, who made an over-the-shoulder reception just beyond the reach of two Auburn defenders. Herron caught Tarkenton's toss at the 2-yard line and strolled into the end zone for the tying touchdown with the extra and winning point to follow.

Whereas the Bulldogs had been fortunate for most of the season, for the majority of the game, it was Auburn that was getting all the breaks. A 15-yard penalty and a fumble by Georgia quarterback Charley Britt had each led to Auburn field goals and a 6–0 halftime lead for the Tigers. Britt redeemed himself with a punt return for a touchdown late in the third quarter, but a possible 10–6 Georgia lead was later squandered with a missed field goal. Midway through the final stanza, Britt was blocked into the kick of his own punter, Bobby Walden. Auburn recovered the botched boot on Georgia's 1-yard line and scored on the next play to take a 13–7 lead.

The Tigers had the ball nearing midfield with only 2:35 remaining and looking to run out the clock. Georgia finally caught a break when guard Pat Dye hit Auburn quarterback Bryant Harvard, forcing a fumble recovered by Dye on the Tigers' 35-yard line.

On first down, Walden attempted a halfback pass that fell incomplete. Tarkenton followed that up with an incompletion of his own. On third and 10, Tarkenton completed a 16-yarder to halfback Don Soberdash down the middle for a first down. From the 19-yard line, Tarkenton passed to Soberdash again for an additional nine yards. However, Tarkenton's next pass fell incomplete, and on third down, his completion to Walden lost three yards.

On fourth down from the 13-yard line, a play came in from the sideline and coach Wally Butts. Tarkenton ignored Butts' called play, knelt on Sanford Stadium's turf, and diagramed the game-winning play.

"I knew we needed something different," Tarkenton later said.

As Tarkenton drifted back, Herron ran downfield, cut to his left, ran past linebacker Jackie Burkett, and slid off defensive back Lamar Rawson. Herron angled into the clear as Tarkenton's pass was thrown to the wide-open receiver.

FRAN TARKENTON

Fran Tarkenton's life both on and off the gridiron following his four years at Georgia has been well documented. During only his sophomore season as a Bulldog, Tarkenton already had begun to exhibit an innovative and risk-taking character that would eventually lead to his success in professional football, as a television personality, and in business.

In his first game on Georgia's varsity against Texas in 1958, Tarkenton claims that, without consulting the Bulldogs coaching staff, he substituted himself for reserve quarterback Tommy Lewis with Georgia trailing the Longhorns 7–0 midway in the third quarter. "[The coaches] wanted to redshirt me, and I didn't want to...so I just bolted onto the field," Tarkenton said years later.

From his own 5-yard line, Tarkenton directed a 21-play, 95-yard drive lasting 8:40 and culminating in a three-yard touchdown pass to Jimmy Vickers. Following the touchdown, coach Wally Butts sent the kicking unit on to try the extra point. Similar to the '59 Auburn game, Butts called for one play but Tarkenton chose another. The sophomore quarterback waved the kicker off the field. Deciding instead to try for two points, Tarkenton passed to Aaron Box for the two-point conversion.

During his 18-season NFL career, the eventual Pro Football Hall of Fame inductee set many records and was regarded as one of the best quarterbacks in the history of the game. After football, Tarkenton appeared on television, wrote books, and became a pioneer in the computer-software business. Currently he markets several services and products, including Tarkenton Financial, Tarkenton Sports and Collectibles, and GoSmallBiz.

Durward Pennington, "the Automatic Toe," converted the extra point, and Georgia led 14–13. After the ensuing kickoff and an Auburn desperation pass falling incomplete, the Bulldogs had clinched their first bowl bid in nine years and the team's first conference title since 1948. Butts and Georgia's assistant coaches were carried to midfield in celebration on the shoulders of the victorious Bulldogs—victory rides that likely would not have occurred if Butts' play had not been disregarded and changed in the huddle by Tarkenton.

Game Details

Georgia 14 • Auburn 13

Date: November 14, 1959

Site: Sanford Stadium

Attendance: 54,000

Records: Georgia 7-1; Auburn 6-1

Rankings: Georgia: No. 12 (AP); Auburn: No. 8 (AP)

Series: Georgia 29-27-6 (Auburn six-game winning streak)

> It was a makeup play, and Tarkenton simply told me to get open. The pass was perfect.
>
> **—Bill Herron, Georgia end**

THE PLAY

Belue-to-Scott 93-yard pass play beats Florida and keeps Georgia's national championship hopes alive

By November 1980, Georgia had soared to a No. 2 ranking in the national polls following eight consecutive victories to begin the season. The Bulldogs had their sights set on a Southeastern Conference title and a Sugar Bowl appearance but, even better, there was the possibility of playing for the school's first undisputed national championship. To be the No. 1 team in the nation and to play for a national title, often a team needs a little luck along the way. The '80 Georgia squad was no different. It needed a great deal of luck during the course of its title run, in particular, on a single play against the University of Florida. Without it, the greatest play in Georgia football history, there would be no top ranking or national championship in 1980.

With only 1:20 remaining in the game, the Bulldogs faced third down and 11 on their own 7-yard line, trailing 21–20 to the Gators. Many Georgia fans had either left or were in the process of departing the Gator Bowl in anticipation of the Bulldogs' first loss of the year. Georgia offensive coordinator George Haffner made the play call with the objective of only getting a first down, 15 to 20 yards at most, to keep the drive alive so

As a corner of Jacksonville's Gator Bowl goes wild, Georgia's Chuck Jones (No. 1) runs in to congratulate and support teammate Lindsay Scott (No. 24), who is getting swarmed by some of the crowd. Scott just accomplished a 93-yard miracle pass play against Florida in 1980—the greatest play in Georgia Bulldogs football history. *Photo courtesy of Hargrett Rare Book & Manuscript Library/University of Georgia Libraries.*

All-American kicker Rex Robinson could eventually be in a position to attempt a game-winning field goal.

Quarterback Buck Belue dropped straight back into the end zone, avoided pressure, and ran to his right nearing the 5-yard line. Split end Lindsay Scott, who had been lined up to Belue's right, had ran a simple curl pattern over the middle. Florida linebacker David Little positioned himself between Belue and Scott. Belue began running away from the pressure and motioned to Scott to slide a little from behind the linebacker. On the run, Belue threw a strike to a leaping Scott, who came down with the reception around the 25-yard line. The junior receiver stumbled a bit upon his catch, regained his balance, turned around, and began heading upfield. As Scott ran toward and then down his left sideline, it appeared several Gators defenders had angles on him to make a play. Scott simply outraced every one of them,

Game Details

Georgia 26 • Florida 21

Date: November 8, 1980

Site: Gator Bowl

Attendance: 68,528

Records: Georgia 8–0; Florida 6–1

Rankings: Georgia: No. 2 (AP)/ No. 2 (UPI); Florida: No. 20 (AP)/ No. 20 (UPI)

Series: Georgia 36–20–2 (Georgia two-game winning streak)

> How could we have given up? There was just too much at stake.
>
> **—Buck Belue, quarterback**

and 93 yards later he was in the end zone for a touchdown. Georgia had somehow miraculously regained a 26–21 advantage over upset-minded Florida.

Because of "the Play," freshman phenomenon Herschel Walker for once was overshadowed, perhaps for the only time during his career at Georgia. Seventy-two of Walker's 238 rushing yards came on a run early in the game and gave the Bulldogs a 7–0 advantage. Georgia held a 20–10 fourth-quarter lead before the Gators, guided by freshman quarterback Wayne Peace, scored 11 consecutive points. Peace's 282 passing yards were the most thrown against the Bulldogs since California's Joe Roth passed for 379 in the 1976 season opener.

NAT HUDSON

As with other great plays in Georgia football history, Buck Belue was obviously an integral part of Georgia's winning play against Florida in 1980. However, it should be noted that without a spectacular block by lineman Nat Hudson, Belue likely would have been sacked in the end zone instead of Lindsay Scott streaking for a touchdown.

In his senior year of 1980, Hudson was in his third consecutive season as a Bulldogs starter along the offensive line. The left guard in 1978 and 1979, Hudson moved to right tackle in '80 and gained 15 pounds to weigh 265—the heaviest among all Georgia starters. Hudson was extremely strong, with lots of endurance and, despite his size, was considered quicker than most linemen.

The unsung hero of "the Play," Hudson slid off his block and to his left when his man dropped into pass coverage. Just as Florida defensive end Mike Clark closed in on Belue a couple of yards into the end zone, Hudson seemingly came out of nowhere to block the hard-charging Clark out of the play. Hudson would eventually be drafted by New Orleans in the sixth round of the 1981 NFL draft. He played 18 games with the Saints and Baltimore for two seasons (1981–1982).

THE PLAY

Needing a miracle, Buck Belue faked a handoff to Herschel Walker and dropped straight back behind his own goal line. Just as Mike Clark converged on the Georgia quarterback, Nat Hudson made a saving block on the Florida defender. The pressure forced Belue to roll out of the end zone and to his right. Spotting a wide-open Lindsay Scott, Belue threw a strike to the receiver at the 25. Running toward the sideline, Scott ran by and away from several Gators defenders, including fallen safety Tim Groves. Once he was near midfield, Scott outraced everyone into the end zone for a touchdown.

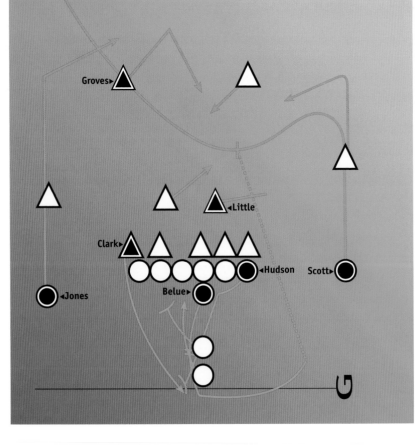

A Mark Dickert punt for Florida went out of bounds on Georgia's 8-yard line with 1:35 to play. On first down, Belue was forced to scramble and lost a yard. On second and 11, Belue's sideline pass to Charles Junior fell incomplete. Just when all hope was lost and the last nail was to be driven in the Dawgs' coffin, Georgia suddenly struck for its 93-yard wonder on third down and long.

The play, also called Left 76 or L-76, had been used by the Bulldogs a couple of times already in the game, but without success. That is, until Georgia tried to execute it one final time. The intent of the play

Quarterback Buck Belue (with football) would have been sacked had it not been for a game-saving block by Nat Hudson (No. 65) against Florida's Mike Clark (No. 87). Belue rolled out to his right and completed a pass to Lindsay Scott on the run. *Photo courtesy of Wingate Downs.*

LINDSAY SCOTT

Lindsay Scott, a highly recruited receiver from Jesup, Georgia, quickly made an impression as a true freshman in 1978. Scott led the Bulldogs in receiving and the conference in kickoff returns and was selected first-team freshman All-American. As a sophomore, Scott again led the team in receiving and kickoff returns. Prior to the 1980 season, Scott's scholarship was rescinded because of an altercation with an academic counselor. By the Florida game, he was no longer the Bulldogs' primary receiver nor was he returning kickoffs. On "the Play," Scott, who later admitted he finally got winded at Florida's 30-yard line, scored his first points since catching a touchdown against the Gators the season before. Following the Florida game and while celebrating the victory, a delighted coach Vince Dooley rightfully said that he "may give [the scholarship] back to [Scott]."

Scott rode his wave of success into his senior season of 1981. His 728 receiving yards were a single-season school record until Andre

Buck Belue (left) and Lindsay Scott (right) embrace after their 93-yard completion stunned Florida and everyone watching. Georgia held on for a 26–21 victory over the Gators, and less than two months later, they capped a perfect 1980 season by winning the national championship. *Photo courtesy of Wingate Downs.*

Hastings' 860 in 1992. Scott was selected both AP and UPI first-team All-SEC. His 2,098 career receiving yards were a school record until 1995 and currently rank eighth.

Scott was the 13th overall pick of the 1982 NFL draft taken by New Orleans. In four seasons and 49 games with the Saints, Scott caught 69 passes, one for a touchdown. Today, he owns a business and lives in Valdosta, Georgia.

was to only gain a first down, and it should have done just that. Safety Tim Groves covered Georgia's Chuck Jones as the flanker ran a long post route. After Belue threw short and Groves drew his attention from Jones to Scott, the Florida safety-man slipped to the Gator Bowl turf. After making the reception, Scott should have been immediately tackled by Groves, but instead, Scott ran by the fallen Gator eventually into the end zone.

As Scott crossed the goal line, bedlam broke out amongst the Bulldogs faithful. Fans, players, photographers, and the like jumped around in the end zone and/or on top of Scott. Items and substances were thrown onto the field in celebration. A sportswriter covering the "World's Largest Outdoor Cocktail Party" later reported it was the first time he had ever been caught in a "liquor storm." Georgia's play-by-play announcer, Larry Munson, got so excited he broke the chair he was sitting on, and the game temporarily went off the air.

Moments after the miracle, Georgia cornerback Mike Fisher intercepted Peace to secure a 26–21 victory.

Later, it was revealed that top-ranked Notre Dame had been tied; Georgia would be the new No. 1 team in college football the following Monday.

Florida head coach Charley Pell later described Belue-to-Scott as a "circus play," while disgruntled Gators receiver Cris Collinsworth added that it was merely a "fluke" and Florida deserved to win. Maybe so, but as defensive coordinator Erk Russell would often say, "I'd rather be lucky than good."

ON THE OFFENSIVE

"THE BIG PLAY" CRIPPLES 'COCKS

Phenomenal reception by Steve "Shag" Davis saves the day against South Carolina

Early on during the 1976 season, if Georgia had been looking past South Carolina to playing Alabama the following week, it was certainly evident as late as four minutes remaining in the third quarter against the Gamecocks. Struggling on offense for most of the game, the Bulldogs trailed and needed a big play in the worst way.

Nicknamed "Shag" because of his shaggy hair, senior receiver Steve Davis had made some remarkable catches before, including a touchdown grab the previous week against Clemson described as "miraculous." However, as quarterback Matt Robinson's long, looping pass drifted toward Shag, it was clear this particular play would not be "big," but rather an overthrown ball falling incomplete.

But, then *it* happened—a moment fittingly headlined by the *Athens Banner-Herald* the next morning as, "The Big Play!"

Enduring a hamstring injury suffered the week of the Clemson game, Davis lunged for Robinson's pass with both arms fully extended, whereupon his fingertips came in contact with the back nose of the ball. Somehow, using only a few tips of his fingers, Davis flicked the ball toward himself, grabbing the back-half of the football with both hands for an astonishing reception. Pulling the ball in, Davis stumbled down inside South Carolina's 10-yard line for a 50-yard gain.

> The Robinson-Davis pass...was clearly the biggest play of the game. The ball may have been overthrown...but Davis chased it down and caught it on his fingertips.
>
> —**Tim Tucker,** *Athens Daily News* **sportswriter**

As South Carolina's Lance Garrett (No. 21) and Bill Currier (No. 24) give pursuit, Steve Davis grabs the pass after first making contact with only his fingertips and flicking the ball into his hands, completing what was called likely the greatest catch in the history of Sanford Stadium. *Photo courtesy of Bob Davis.*

What was then called "brilliant" would remain a head scratcher decades later for Georgia coaching legend Vince Dooley: "To this day, I *still* don't know how Shag caught that!"

En route to what would be a 10–1 regular season and a Sugar Bowl appearance against Pittsburgh for the national title, Dooley's Dogs had opened their 1976 campaign with impressive victories over the nationally-ranked California Golden Bears followed by a 41–0 rout at Clemson. Looming as the fourth game on the schedule was a meeting with mighty Alabama, which was already being considered perhaps the most important home game in UGA football history. But first, the Bulldogs had to host the Gamecocks, a familiar foe though not much of a rival at the time.

Game Details

Georgia 20 • South Carolina 12

Date: September 25, 1976

Site: Sanford Stadium

Attendance: 59,925

Records: Georgia 2-0; South Carolina 3-0

Rankings: Georgia 7th AP/7th UPI

Series: Georgia 24-4-2 (Georgia eight-game winning streak)

> It had to be an act of God that I caught that football. I was probably the most shocked guy in the stadium that I made the catch.
>
> **—Steve Davis, Georgia receiver**

With South Carolina holding a 12–7 advantage, the Gamecock defense forced Georgia to bog down once again inside its own territory. Facing third down on their 41-yard line, the Bulldogs called for Robinson to throw to Davis, who was to line up at a tight end position.

After racing straight down the hash marks at full speed, Davis looked straight up above him just as the ball arrived. He lunged in full

STEVE DAVIS

According to the FWAA, Steve Davis of Cambridge, Maryland, had been the best high school senior quarterback in all of America in 1971 before he arrived at the University of Georgia the following fall. After sustaining an injury early on, he was moved to receiver and wound up leading Georgia's 1972 freshman team in receiving. However, suspensions and injuries would soon plague Davis until his senior season of 1976.

After being kicked off the team in 1973 for disciplinary reasons, Davis was one of the leading receivers in the SEC early in the 1974 season before he was suspended again. For the next season and a half, Davis either played a reserve role or was injured, and only made a handful of receptions. Finally, in his fifth-year senior campaign of 1976, Davis' talent became evident. Through the first four games of the year, he led the team in receiving, and again was one of the conference's leading receivers, until a Georgia loss at Ole Miss influenced the Bulldogs to recommit to their ground-attack offense.

Despite starting only 14 games while making just 24 receptions for his Georgia career, Davis was the third Bulldog selected in the 1977 NFL draft (and, the two Georgia players chosen before him had been first-team All-Americans in 1976). He attended NFL training camps with the Houston Oilers in 1977 and New York Giants in 1979. Above all, according to Vince Dooley, Davis had the "best hands" of any player he had ever seen during his 25 years as Georgia's head coach.

anticipation of the ball sailing beyond his hands, but ended up being "just lucky, I guess" he'd later claim.

Davis' phenomenal catch seemed to spark the entire Georgia team. Soon, Robinson passed to running back Al Pollard for a nine-yard touchdown. In the fourth quarter, Kevin McLee's touchdown run gave the Bulldogs a 20–12 lead. Late in the contest, the Gamecocks advanced inside Georgia's 10-yard line, hoping to tie the game; however, the Bulldogs' Bobby Thompson recovered a fumble, securing the eight-point win for Georgia.

"As I was walking off the field after the game, this elderly man came up to me," Davis said. "He said that he had been coming to

VINCE DOOLEY

When a 31-year-old Dooley was hired as Georgia's head coach in December 1963, it amazed just about everyone. Quarterback and future All-American safety Lynn Hughes said years later, "We were sitting on the steps at Stegeman [Hall] wondering 'Who the hell is Vince Dooley?'"

Dooley's celebrated coaching career would include many accolades, namely, 201 victories, six SEC titles, a national championship in 1980, and coaching the Bulldogs to the best overall record in all of college football from 1980 to 1983 (43-4-1). However, sometimes overlooked, Dooley enjoyed plenty of success at Georgia prior to the early 1980s, especially against first-rate opposition.

Consider that prior to Dooley's arrival, Georgia teams had been a dreadful 2-25-1 against AP-ranked opponents from 1951 through 1963. However, from the middle of his very first season through the 1968 regular season, Dooley's Dogs went undefeated against 10 ranked opponents.

For the 1976 regular season, the legendary head coach was undefeated again versus ranked teams—a perfect 4-0—and, by that time, hardly anyone was still left wondering, "Who was Vince Dooley?"

Georgia games since the stadium was built [in 1929] and he had never seen a better catch." The day after the Bulldogs' victory, a newspaper writer agreed with the man, declaring Davis' reception was "likely the greatest catch in the history of Sanford Stadium." Yet, because the catch was not made by a household name, did not occur late in a game, did not directly result in victory, and was not even a scoring play, even some of the most knowledgeable of UGA football historians are totally unaware of it.

Nevertheless, "The Big Play" from Davis was actually something much more than a great play. Without it, there is arguably no win over South Carolina. And, without a victory over the Gamecocks, which preceded what would be a historic 21–0 triumph over Alabama, Georgia would not have played for the national championship on New Year's Day of 1977.

The week prior to his remarkable catch against South Carolina, Steve Davis made two touchdown receptions at Clemson: a "miraculous" nine-yarder, and this 36-yard pass and run for a score. *Photo courtesy of Bob Davis.*

EXCESSIVE BUT EFFECTIVE CELEBRATION

Penalty called on Georgia following a Knowshon Moreno touchdown unifies young Bulldogs squad

In 2007 a favored Georgia squad traveled to face Tennessee in Knoxville, where it was surprisingly dominated and defeated by three touchdowns. It next survived a scare in Nashville only when a late fumble by Vanderbilt saved the Bulldogs from losing for a second consecutive week. Georgia needed a field goal by Brandon Coutu in the final seconds to defeat the Commodores, 20–17.

A much-needed week off followed for Georgia before its yearly journey to Jacksonville to meet the Florida Gators. Since 1990 the Bulldogs had lost 15 of 17 games to Florida. The Gators were nationally ranked in the top 10 and coming off a national championship in 2006. A loss to Florida by Georgia's young and inexperienced squad seemed certain, and some Bulldogs backers were already looking past the seemingly disappointing 2007 season and ahead to '08.

Florida took the opening kickoff and quickly moved from its 29-yard line to Georgia's 33 before

Nearly every Bulldog stormed the field to celebrate in the end zone following the first score of the 2007 Georgia-Florida game. Georgia's celebration resulted in a couple of penalties but arguably revitalized its season. *Photo courtesy of AP Images.*

losing a fumble to cornerback Asher Allen. After Allen's return to the Gators' 39, the Bulldogs executed eight consecutive running plays, seven by tailback Knowshon Moreno, to Florida's 1-yard line. On third down and goal, quarterback Matthew Stafford turned to his right and handed the ball to Moreno for the eighth time. Moreno ran directly up the middle and dove for the end zone, barely breaking the plane of the goal line for a touchdown. With six minutes remaining in the opening quarter, the Bulldogs had struck first.

Suddenly, most of Georgia's sideline emptied onto the field to join the offensive unit. There were approximately 70 Bulldogs celebrating the game's first touchdown as Florida players looked on in bewilderment. Many witnesses, including Florida coach Urban Meyer, thought a fight had broken out, but on the contrary, a party had started. The highlights of Georgia's jubilation were left tackle Trinton Sturdivant's dancing and center Fernando Velasco pretending to take photos of Moreno posing in the end zone. The exuberant end zone celebration was certainly a first at Georgia, if not in all of organized football.

KNOWSHON MORENO

Although considered Georgia's third-string tailback during the summer of 2007, Knowshon Moreno was being compared, even by Coach Richt, to Georgia great Garrison Hearst. However, at the time only Herschel Walker—not Hearst—had a better and more impactful freshman campaign than the New Jersey native Moreno did in 2007.

Moreno was not Georgia's third tailback for long after carrying the ball 20 times and catching two passes in the season opener against Oklahoma State. His 22 touches against the Cowboys would be his most until Georgia's seventh game, versus Vanderbilt.

For the Bulldogs' next five games, Moreno was one of college football's premier backs, averaging more than 153 rushing yards on 26 carries per game while scoring a total of nine touchdowns. He finished the season with 1,334 rushing yards, a 5.4 rushing average, 14 touchdowns, and 20 catches. He was the only Bulldog in 2007 named to both the Associated Press and Coaches All-SEC first teams, and he was also selected to several freshman All-American first teams. In 2008, he led the SEC in rushing as a sophomore before being drafted by the Denver Broncos.

Knowshon Moreno scores his first touchdown against the Gators on a one-yard run. He would account for two additional touchdowns while rushing for 188 yards on 33 carries. *Photo courtesy of AP Images.*

With several penalty flags strewn across the field, most of the Bulldogs retreated back to the sideline for Coutu to attempt the extra point. After Coutu's successful kick, Georgia was forced to kick off from its 7½-yard line instead of the 30. The 22½ yards in penalties were well worth it.

MARK RICHT

After achieving an 8–4 record in his inaugural season as a head coach in 2001, Mark Richt's next four Georgia teams (2002–2005) each won 10 or more games and finished ranked 10th or higher in both major polls. After not appearing in the first 10 years of the SEC Championship Game, the Bulldogs played for the title three times during the four-year span, winning twice. In 2006 Georgia rebounded from a 6–4 start to end the season with three consecutive victories over ranked opponents and to finish with a 9–4 record and a No. 23 ranking. Richt's 2007 team was similar to the previous year's version as the Bulldogs struggled during the middle of the season but finished extremely strong, beginning with a victory over Florida.

The usually conservative and mild-mannered Richt certainly acted out of character with his motivational directive against the Gators. Soon afterward, the coach's integrity was exhibited when he contacted SEC commissioner Mike Slive to apologize for his actions.

Relieving himself of play-calling duties beginning with the 2006 Georgia Tech game, Richt has more time to spend on the intangibles of football and was likely more acquainted with his team than in the past. Richt knew exactly what might be instrumental in enhancing the intensity level of his squad. It can be argued that the coach's ordered celebration was a major factor in Georgia achieving one of its best seasons; only one other time in history has the Bulldogs' 2007 No. 2 national ranking in the AP poll been matched or exceeded—the 1980 national championship.

Following the game, some questioned Georgia's discipline, class, and poise. One member of the media went so far as to call it "foolishness."

The Bulldogs' hoopla following the game's first score did not secure victory for Georgia. In fact, the Gators would tie the score only three plays and 1:21 later on a 40-yard pass from quarterback Tim Tebow to Louis Murphy. What the celebration did was unify and motivate a young Bulldogs team. This particular Georgia squad wanted to demonstrate it was different from the previous ones the Gators were used to dominating.

Coach Mark Richt had ordered the celebration, telling his offense that if they did not receive a penalty after their first touchdown, he would run them at 5:45 AM the following week. Richt wanted to fire up

Game Details

Georgia 42 • Florida 30

Date: October 27, 2007

Site: Jacksonville Municipal Stadium

Attendance: 84,481

Records: Georgia 5-2; Florida 5-2

Rankings: Georgia: No. 20 (AP)/ No. 19 (USA Today); Florida: No. 9 (AP)/ No. 11 (USA Today)

Series: Georgia 46-37-2 (Florida two-game winning streak)

> I told [the team] we are going to liven it up and create some excitement.
>
> **—Mark Richt, Georgia head coach**

THE CELEBRATION

Quarterback Matthew Stafford signaled with his left foot, and fullback Shaun Chapas went into motion from his left to right. Stafford turned and handed the football to Knowshon Moreno, who got the football at the 6. Moreno took three steps and leaped from the 3 over a pile of players. Moreno's outstretched football barely broke the plane of Florida's goal line for the first score of the contest. Suddenly and unexpectedly, almost the entire Georgia team ran from the sideline and gathered with the offense in the end zone for a celebration unlike anything ever witnessed before in football.

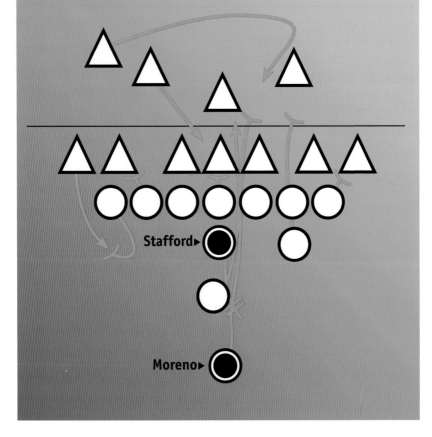

> That's what [the team] did [following the game's first touchdown]. They just ran out there and formed a big, old Dog Pile.
>
> **—Marcus Howard, Georgia defensive end**

his young players and generate greater intensity; however, he did not realize nearly the entire team would participate in the celebration.

After Florida had tied the game at 7–7, Georgia answered two plays later on an 84-yard touchdown pass from Stafford to Mohamed Massaquoi. The Bulldogs would go on to shock the seven-and-a-half-point-favored Gators 42–30. Moreno was outstanding, rushing for 188 yards and three touchdowns on 33 carries. Georgia's defense recorded six sacks of Tebow, who had been sacked just five times all season.

Moreno's first touchdown against Florida and the excessive celebration that followed arguably turned around a season that had appeared to be heading nowhere fast. Beginning with the Florida victory, the Bulldogs played like a different team through the end of the year, finishing with seven consecutive victories, winning the Sugar Bowl, and ranking second in the nation in the final Associated Press Poll.

Sometimes unexpected occurrences can unite and motivate young men to overcome apparently insurmountable obstacles to succeed. For the Bulldogs in 2007, it seems "foolishness" led to greater successes.

FAIRGROUND GALLANTRY

Red and Black escape upset with Bob McWhorter's late touchdown pass

The eighth annual Georgia-Carolina State Fair was 11 days of corn, kennel, livestock, and poultry shows, automobile and motorcycle races, and an "auto-polo game: one of the most thrilling events ever witnessed on earth." Held at Augusta, Georgia's fairgrounds, the fair was considered one of the best agricultural festivals in the South.

Played on the second day of the gala, the 1913 Georgia-Clemson contest was thought to be only a small part of the celebration; however, the football game, a specific touchdown pass in particular, turned out to be one of the most thrilling events in Georgia football history at that point in time.

Losing 15–12 with only a few minutes left in the game, Georgia All-American Bob McWhorter lofted a long pass to newcomer Roy "Scrapper" Smith, who caught the ball on the 1-yard line and crossed Clemson's goal for the game-winning score. The pass play ended any hopes for a Clemson upset, added to McWhorter's illustrious career as perhaps the most valuable Georgia football player of all time, and was the pinnacle

In 1913 Bob McWhorter was selected as Georgia's first All-American. Known primarily as a gifted runner, McWhorter helped defeat Clemson that season by throwing two long touchdowns to Roy Smith, the second coming in the closing minutes of the ballgame.
Photo courtesy of Hargrett Rare Book & Manuscript Library/University of Georgia Libraries.

in the football career of Smith, a little-known end at Georgia until his acclaimed scoring catch.

In large part because of coach Alex Cunningham's stellar guidance and halfback McWhorter's outstanding play, by 1913 Georgia was considered one of the best teams in the South. After nearly two decades of mediocrity since they began playing football in 1892, the Red and Black had contended for the Southern Intercollegiate Athletic Association (SIAA) championship every year since 1910. Unsuccessful in capturing the SIAA title since 1896, Georgia had only lost to an excellent Virginia team in '13 and was believed to be able to easily handle an average Clemson squad.

From the onset, Clemson was shockingly able to move the ball easily against Georgia while holding McWhorter and the rest of the Red and

DAVE PADDOCK

Dave Paddock, a New Yorker tired of northern winters, came to the University of Georgia and tried out for football in 1912. Barely making the squad, he moved positions from halfback to quarterback by the end of the season. It was at Paddock's new position that he starred with his quickness and shifty moves.

Although he was not directly involved in Georgia's memorable, game-winning touchdown pass to defeat Clemson in 1913, if it were not for Paddock, the Red and Black likely would have lost. Paddock gained 165 of Georgia's 318 rushing yards, averaged 15 yards per carry, and had two runs of 40-yard gains.

In 1914 Paddock scored his first touchdown at Georgia against North Carolina. At the conclusion of the season, he was named the school's second All-American by the *New York Herald*.

Paddock scored four touchdowns in 1915, including one in his final game at Georgia, a 13–0 win over Clemson. He was later selected the first-team quarterback for Georgia's all-time team prior to World War I (1891–1916).

Black offense to short gains. Soon after Clemson's J.P. Jeter missed a field goal, teammate Johnny Logan booted one from the 25-yard line to give the underdogs a 3–0 lead.

Shortly thereafter, McWhorter caught a missed field goal on his goal line and ran 20 yards before fumbling and losing the ball. On the next play, Clemson's quarterback, Jimmie James, ran for a touchdown. The extra point was missed, but Clemson held a commanding 9–0 advantage.

After a scoreless second quarter, Georgia quarterback Dave Paddock broke loose for one of his four runs of 20 yards or more during the game; he would finish with an impressive 165 yards on 11 carries. On the next play, McWhorter scored on a short run, and Georgia finally had some points.

Into the final quarter, Clemson had scored again. Georgia trailed 15–6 and was seemingly to lose only its sixth of 32 games since Cunningham and McWhorter's arrival. It seemed that it would take a miracle for the Red and Black to snatch victory out of the jaws of defeat, something McWhorter had accomplished before.

Game Details

Georgia 18 • Clemson 15

Date: November 6, 1913

Site: Augusta Fairgrounds

Attendance: 6,000 (attendance at Georgia-Carolina State Fair)

Records: Georgia 4–1; Clemson 2–2

Series: Clemson 8-7-1 (Georgia two-game winning streak)

> We expected a hard game, and we got it.
>
> **—Bob McWhorter, standout Georgia halfback**

ROY "SCRAPPER" SMITH

Roy Smith's first and only season at the University of Georgia was in 1913. Playing from his end position, he weighed a scant 145 pounds but reportedly was extremely fast. Although Smith started in six of the Red and Black's eight games (three at left end, three at right end), he is scarcely mentioned in Georgia's football archives. The only points he scored in 1913 were 12 on the two come-from-behind touchdown receptions from Bob McWhorter against Clemson. While playing football at Georgia, Scrapper was a true "two-hit wonder."

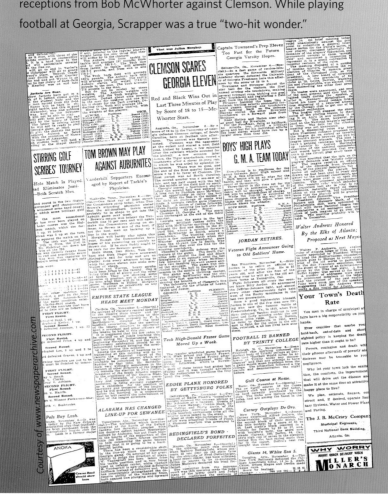

Courtesy of www.newspaperarchive.com

Clemson had limited McWhorter's rushing; he would finish the game gaining only 75 yards on 21 carries with just two runs greater than five yards. However, Clemson had yet to face his passing prowess. Although Clemson allowed Georgia only one completion in its first nine passing attempts, only two of the tosses were thrown by McWhorter.

Facing third down on Clemson's 30-yard line, McWhorter connected with Smith for a touchdown, and Georgia had pulled within three points.

In the last few minutes of the contest, Tanny Webb punted to McWhorter, who was immediately tackled. On the next play, McWhorter threw again to Smith and again got the same result. Smith caught the pass on the 1-yard line and crossed Clemson's goal for a 45-yard touchdown, giving Georgia an 18–15 lead. The Red and Black missed the extra-point attempt, but it would not matter.

Clemson had one last possession, but on Georgia's kickoff, Logan fumbled and the Red and Black recovered on the 40-yard line. Georgia ran five plays, gaining 15 yards, before the game ended.

At perhaps the grandest agricultural exhibition in the South, behind the arm of McWhorter and the hands of Smith, the Red and Black's fierce rally was one of the most illustrious comebacks ever witnessed on a Southern gridiron.

NO LONGER NO. 1

Tim Worley's dazzling 89-yard run caps Bulldogs' stunning defeat of top-ranked Florida

In 1985 Georgia made its annual trek to Jacksonville, Florida, for the "World's Largest Outdoor Cocktail Party" and met a University of Florida team like no other before. The Gators were on an 18-game nonlosing streak and were ranked No. 1 in the nation for the first time in school history.

Florida had no apparent weaknesses. It had a dominating defense and a highly productive offense. The Gators' quarterback, sophomore Kerwin Bell, was the second-highest-rated passer in the nation and a Heisman Trophy candidate. Florida's massive and preeminent offensive line was nicknamed the "Great Wall of Florida."

A victory over Georgia seemed so certain that, days before the contest, the Jacksonville Gator Club printed and distributed flyers advertising a postgame victory party at the Jacksonville Coliseum immediately following Florida's win. The Gators were aiming for a national championship, and the Bulldogs were expected to be their next opponent to fall by the wayside.

Tim Worley outraces Florida's Curtis Stacy into the end zone, completing an 89-yard touchdown run. Worley's lengthy jaunt clinched an upset victory over the Gators and still remains tied as the longest scoring rush in school history. *Photo courtesy of Wingate Downs.*

However, it would be the Gators suffering defeat and falling from the Associated Press Poll's pinnacle spot. Freshman Tim Worley's spectacular 89-yard touchdown jaunt capped an improbable three-touchdown victory for the Bulldogs. Worley's lengthy run tied a school record and was the highlight of the tailback's outstanding career at Georgia, one that included a run for the Heisman Trophy in 1988 as a junior.

In the opening stanza, freshman fullback Keith Henderson streaked up the middle through Florida's dominating defense for a 76-yard score. In the next quarter, Henderson did the same thing, on the exact same play, for a 32-yard touchdown, and Georgia surprisingly led 14–0 and later 17–3 at halftime. Florida's Bell drove the Gators all over the field but could never cross Georgia's goal line. He finished the game with a school-record 408 passing yards on 33 of 49 passing; however, he lost a fumble and also threw an interception. As far as Florida's "Great Wall," it allowed Bell to get sacked five times while paving the way for Gators rushers to gain a meager 28 yards on 30 carries.

Late in the game, Florida was threatening to score, but John L. Williams lost a fumble. Linebacker Steve Boswell recovered the ball on Georgia's own 8-yard line. On first down, Henderson carried for three yards to the 11-yard line.

TIM WORLEY

As a freshman in 1985, Tim Worley, along with Keith Henderson, Lars Tate, David McCluskey, and James Jackson, was part of a dynamic quintet of Bulldogs rushers who each entered the Florida game averaging at least 40 rushing yards per game for the season. Worley would finish the year second on the team with 627 rushing yards and first with 10 touchdowns.

Against Florida in 1985, Worley carried the ball just seven times for 104 yards, 89 of which came on his memorable run. According to Georgia's offensive coaching staff, Worley's long jaunt was more important than Henderson's two scoring sprints. Before the 89-yard score, the Gators were only one play from cutting their deficit to a touchdown. In addition, Worley's late touchdown clinched Georgia's only win ever over a top-ranked team.

Worley's 1986 season was cut short because of an injury, and he was redshirted as a junior. In '88 Worley rebounded to rush for 1,216 yards, was responsible for 20 touchdowns, was named first-team All-American, and was a Heisman Trophy candidate until the final couple weeks of the season. He still ranks high in several all-time career categories at Georgia despite playing in only 26 regular-season games.

Crossing Florida's goal line, Worley celebrates as his spectacular run increases the Bulldogs' lead to three touchdowns. *Photo courtesy of Wingate Downs.*

KEITH HENDERSON

For the 1985 season freshman Keith Henderson led the Bulldogs in rushing, including 145 yards on nine carries and the two long scoring runs against Florida. Against the Gators, he spearheaded a rushing attack that gained 344 yards and averaged 7.3 yards per carry. Entering the game, Florida had the 10th-best rushing defense in the nation, allowing just 105 yards per game and 2.8 yards per carry.

Like Tim Worley, Henderson missed part of the '86 season with an injury, was redshirted in 1987, and left one year early for the NFL following the '88 season. Despite playing fewer than three seasons and leaving the school two decades ago, Henderson remains among the top 20 at Georgia in career all-purpose yardage.

Due primarily to Keith Henderson's 145 rushing yards and two touchdowns, Florida was upset 24-3 in 1985 and fell from its No. 1 ranking. *Photo courtesy of Wingate Downs.*

On the next play, the Bulldogs ran a toss sweep with Worley to the right side. He ran through a huge hole created by the offensive line. Suddenly, a Gators defender grabbed at Worley's leg and nearly tore his shoe off. The shoe slipped from the heel but luckily slipped back on the foot with the next running stride. Distancing himself from Florida's defense, Worley ran down the sideline and then cut back around the Gators' 40-yard line toward the middle of the field. Here, the tailback outran the last would-be tackler, cornerback Curtis Stacy, for an 89-yard touchdown with 3:58 left on the clock.

Worley's magnificent, 89-yard sprint is still tied with Johnny Griffith's run in 1946 versus Furman for the longest rushing touchdown at Georgia. Most importantly, Worley's accomplishment put the final nail in the top-ranked Gators' coffin in a 24–3 upset victory for the Dogs in what remains the lone win in Georgia football history over a No. 1–ranked team.

Game Details

Georgia 24 • Florida 3

Date: November 9, 1985

Site: Gator Bowl

Attendance: 82,327

Records: Georgia 6–1–1; Florida 7–0–1

Rankings: Georgia: No. 17 (AP)/ No. 15 (UPI); Florida: No. 1 (AP)

Series: Georgia 40–21–2 (Florida one-game winning streak)

> Georgia played one of its greatest games ever today.... I don't know how you play any better. Everybody was superb.
>
> **—Vince Dooley, Georgia head coach**

THERE GOES HERSCHEL!

Freshman Walker outraces entire Gamecocks defense for a breathtaking 76-yard touchdown

Georgia and South Carolina both had surpassed most expectations by November 1980. The Bulldogs were undefeated and ranked fourth in the nation. Unranked in the preseason, the Gamecocks had lost only to Southern California and were positioned at No. 14 by the pollsters. The Georgia–South Carolina meeting had garnered enough attention around the country to televise the event—only the third game ever nationally televised in Athens. Although the Dogs and 'Cocks were considered an appealing matchup, most of the national media would not have come to Athens if not for the clash between players who were probably college football's best two running backs.

South Carolina's George Rogers was primarily responsible for the Gamecocks' best record since 1924. Rogers, a Georgia native, had already rushed for more than 1,000 yards in only seven games and was the odds-on favorite to receive the Heisman Trophy. The senior running back had always performed well against Georgia,

Herschel Walker slides off right tackle, heading toward the sideline against South Carolina in 1980. The freshman tailback outraced the entire Gamecocks defense, gaining 76 yards for a touchdown. *Photo courtesy of Wingate Downs.*

rushing for 310 yards on 66 carries in three games since 1977. He was also the key reason why South Carolina had defeated the Bulldogs two consecutive years.

The highly recruited Herschel Walker chose Georgia over the rest of the nation and instantly made a tremendous impact. Although he had played sparingly in the fourth and fifth games of the season, Walker had rushed for 877 yards in seven contests, ranking ninth in the country in rushing. Herschel quickly made a name for himself by scoring on long runs. He had already rushed for four touchdowns of 48 yards or more, including a 76-yarder against Texas A&M. However, the freshman phenom's best run was yet to come.

Early in the third quarter, with Georgia leading 3–0, the Bulldogs had possession on their own 24-yard line. Walker took a delayed handoff from quarterback Buck Belue on a play designed to be run through the right portion of the offensive line. Instead, Walker slid off right tackle. Aided by fullback Jimmy Womack's crushing block on a Gamecocks linebacker, Walker headed toward his right sideline and was off to the races. As he dashed down the sideline, three different South Carolina defenders had perfect angles to intercept the fast-moving freshman. However, never before had college football seen a back combine such speed, size, and power. Walker was not to be caught,

Game Details

Georgia 13 • South Carolina 10

Date: November 1, 1980

Site: Sanford Stadium

Attendance: 62,200

Records: Georgia 7–0; South Carolina 6–1

Rankings: Georgia: No. 4 (AP)/ No. 4 (UPI); South Carolina: No. 14 (AP)/ No. 14 (UPI)

Series: Georgia 26–6–2 (South Carolina two-game winning streak)

> There was not another back in the game who could have scored on that play.
>
> **—Vince Dooley, Georgia head coach**

leaving the last would-be tackler 15 yards behind him on his way to a 76-yard touchdown.

At halftime, the Bulldogs held a 3–0 lead. According to Coach Vince Dooley, it should have been by more, but poor coaching decisions and a missed 22-yard field-goal attempt had cost Georgia a wider scoring margin.

Georgia took the second-half kickoff and, from its own 20-yard line, gained four yards in two plays. Faced with third down and 6, Tailback Draw 22 was the play called, and Walker responded with his long jaunt to pay dirt. What makes Walker's run so remarkable was the fact that he

HERSCHEL WALKER

Herschel Walker's 219-yard rushing performance against South Carolina in 1980 instantly propelled him into the running for the Heisman Trophy. After rushing for a combined 315 yards against Florida and Auburn, Walker would finish third in the trophy's voting. His 205 yards and three touchdowns against Georgia Tech in the regular-season finale were unfortunately not considered because the votes had already been submitted. If Walker's performance against Georgia Tech had been considered prior to the voting, he might have been accorded the Heisman, even though he was only a freshman.

Walker followed up his sensational freshman season with second- and first-place Heisman Trophy finishes in 1981 and 1982, respectively. His third-second-first Heisman finishes are unprecedented and one of many reasons why he is Georgia's greatest player ever, if not college football's greatest. Most importantly, Walker was the catalyst for the Bulldogs' success from 1980 to 1982, when they achieved a 33–3 record and won three Southeastern Conference titles and a national championship.

Since retiring from professional football after the 1997 season, Walker has been involved in a variety of business opportunities. Currently, he owns and operates Renaissance Man Food Services.

Running out of the I formation, Herschel Walker took the handoff from quarterback Buck Belue and followed fullback Jimmy Womack through a hole on the right side of the line. Walker then turned upfield along the sideline and outraced three South Carolina defenders on his way to the end zone.

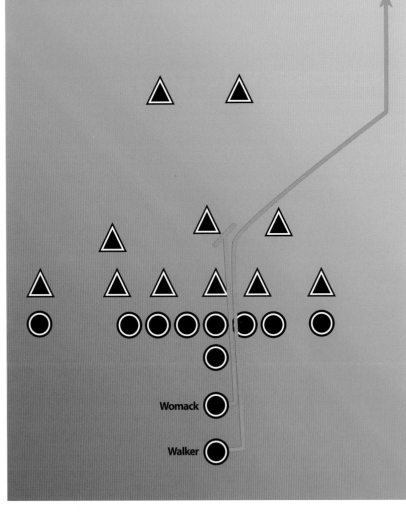

outran three Gamecocks who each could have taken him down—that is, if he was any other ordinary running back.

The fact that Walker first outran left cornerback Harry Skipper, South Carolina's fastest player, should have been indicative that no one would catch him. Next, free safety Robert Perlotte had an angle to catch him but could not. Finally, right cornerback Mark Bridges was left in the tailback's dust.

Georgia would lead 13–0 before the Gamecocks stormed back and trailed by only three points late in the third quarter. With 5:22 left in the contest and South Carolina threatening to at least tie the game, Rogers, who finished with 168 yards on 35 carries, lost a fumble that was recovered by the Bulldogs on their own 16-yard line. Georgia would eventually run out the clock and defeat the 'Cocks, 13–10.

Walker outdid Rogers by rushing for 219 yards on a school-record 43 carries. When asked after the game which player, Walker or Rogers, he would rather have on his team, Dooley replied: "They are both great backs, but I'll take Herschel. For one thing, he has three more years to play."

Herschel would play two more seasons following 1980 before departing early for the professional ranks. In becoming perhaps college football's greatest player ever, Walker had several lengthy touchdown runs that helped distinguish his outstanding collegiate career. None of them were more memorable than his 76-yarder against South Carolina in 1980.

> I surprised myself [with the 76-yard scoring run]. I didn't know I had that kind of ability.
>
> **—Herschel Walker, tailback**

POSCHNER PROPELS BULLDOGS TO NO. 1

George Poschner's acrobatic reception from Frank Sinkwich defeats Alabama in '42

After nearly a decade of mediocrity, Georgia football began making great strides in the early 1940s. In 1942 Coach Wally Butts had a stellar senior class, featuring All-Americans Frank Sinkwich (halfback) and George Poschner (end), that led the Bulldogs to an unblemished record through six games and a No. 2 national ranking. Playing at the neutral site of Atlanta's Grant Field because gas rationing was in effect during World War II, Georgia faced third-ranked Alabama. The undefeated Crimson Tide had been chosen national champions by the Houlgate System the previous season and looked to duplicate this achievement in 1942. Georgia hoped to defeat Alabama for the first time in 13 years in a game that had been sold out for nearly a month.

In the fourth quarter, the Bulldogs had rallied and cut their deficit to three points,

All-American George Poschner caught two touchdown passes from Frank Sinkwich—
including one while "standing on his head"—in a 21-10 victory over Alabama in 1942.

Photo courtesy of Hargrett Rare Book & Manuscript Library/University of Georgia Libraries.

10–7. The Crimson Tide defense had slowed the great Sinkwich's running (he finished with only 39 rushing yards on 20 carries), but the eventual Heisman Trophy recipient's aerial attack suddenly could not be stopped. Georgia had a second down and 11 on Alabama's 15-yard line. Sinkwich fired a pass down the middle near the goal line. Just as Poschner made a leaping catch between two Crimson Tide defenders, he was hit both high and low. Georgia's magnificent left end completely turned a flip in the air and came down on his head and one shoulder. Poschner rolled into the end zone, clutching the football to his chest. It was an extraordinary, acrobatic catch for a touchdown made by one of the best ends in football.

FRANK SINKWICH

Frank Sinkwich's performance on the gridiron is well documented. He finished fourth in the Heisman Trophy voting as a junior when he became the first player in the history of college football to amass 2,000 yards of total offense. As a senior, he was the Heisman recipient and ended a collegiate football career that still remains one of the very best at the University of Georgia.

Few realize that Sinkwich almost did not come to Georgia but nearly attended Ohio State University. When coach Wally Butts recruited the prep star from Youngstown, Ohio, Sinkwich insisted that Butts also give a scholarship to his hometown friend, George Poschner. Butts was not overly impressed with Poschner but wanted Sinkwich so badly, he offered scholarships to both Youngstown natives.

After a short stint with the U.S. Marines, Sinkwich was the first selection of the 1943 NFL draft. By his second season in the professional ranks, Sinkwich was named the NFL's Most Valuable Player in 1944, playing for the Detroit Lions. However, by 1947, because of a knee injury, his football career had ended. Sinkwich was a successful businessman for years until his death in 1990.

Georgia had dedicated the game to its former center, Tommy Witt, who had died during the early stages of the war. In the second half and with Alabama holding a 10–0 lead, someone sarcastically stated in Georgia's offensive huddle how proud Witt must have been of his Bulldogs teammates' performance thus far. The remark "was like a message from God," Sinkwich said years later. "The effect was electrical—everyone felt it."

Georgia's offense suddenly came alive as Sinkwich completed five of six passes for 77 yards. The final completion was a five-yard touchdown toss early in the final quarter to Poschner, who made the scoring catch just beyond the reach of defensive back Al Sabo.

Later in the quarter, Alabama's Norm "Monk" Mosley was forced to quick kick from his own territory. Earlier in the game, Mosley's first quick kick had traveled 78 yards and pinned Georgia near its own goal line. However, Mosley's second kick, the turning point of the contest,

Game Details

Georgia 21 • Alabama 10

Date: October 31, 1942

Site: Grant Field

Attendance: 32,000

Records: Georgia 6-0; Alabama 5-0

Rankings: Georgia: No. 2 (AP); Alabama: No. 3 (AP)

Series: Alabama 14-11-3 (Alabama four-game winning streak)

> We stopped [the Bulldogs] running, but we couldn't check that passing attack.
>
> **—Frank Thomas, Alabama head coach**

landed on the Bulldogs' 30-yard line, but instead of rolling for additional yardage, bounced straight up in the air and backward two yards. Georgia took over on its own 32-yard line, trailing 10–7.

On first down, Sinkwich passed to Van Davis, who lateraled to Ken Keuper, who streaked to the Crimson Tide's 48-yard line. From there, "Fireball" Frankie Sinkwich completed a 24-yard pass to Poschner. From Alabama's 24-yard line, Sinkwich threw incomplete but followed it up with an eight-yard completion to Davis. On third and two from the

GEORGE POSCHNER

If not for Frank Sinkwich, George Poschner would not have been a Georgia Bulldog. A skinny, 150-pound recruit one year removed from high school, Poschner grew to a 180-pound All-American end by 1942. After breaking his arm against the University of Alabama as a junior, Poschner retaliated against the Crimson Tide with his two-touchdown performance in 1942. The Youngstown, Ohio, native was also an outstanding defender. On Alabama's possession after Poschner's unbelievable touchdown grab, he sacked Norm "Monk" Mosley for a seven-yard loss, which led to Andy Dudish's fumble return for a score. In the same game, writer Bill Cunningham wrote that when Poschner "hit his man you could see Crimson legs in the air."

In three seasons (1940–1942) on Georgia's varsity, Poschner scored 10 touchdowns, nine receiving and one by recovering a nonreturned kickoff, and he scored 61 career points. Six of his touchdowns were scored in his senior All-American campaign.

Poschner followed his friend Sinkwich from high school to Georgia and then again to the NFL when he too was drafted by the Detroit Lions in 1943 (eighth round, 61st overall pick). However, he never played professionally. Poschner was soon partially paralyzed and lost both legs because of injuries sustained in the Battle of the Bulge in World War II. Nevertheless, one of college football's greatest ends during his time lived to be 85 years old until his death in 2005.

16-yard line, Sinkwich rushed for two yards and a critical first down. On first down, Sinkwich lost a yard back to the 15.

Next, Poschner made his second touchdown reception while "standing on his head." How Poschner held on to the football, no one knows, but it gave Georgia its first lead of the ballgame.

On the ensuing possession, Georgia added an additional score for good measure. Alabama's Russ Craft was hit by Walter Maguire and fumbled. Andy Dudish of Georgia grabbed the midair fumble and ran 19 yards into the end zone.

Although he had his worst rushing performance in quite some time in the 21–10 win, Sinkwich completed 17 of 32 passes for 222 yards, including nine of 11 for 154 yards on Georgia's two rallying touchdown drives.

The 1942 Alabama game has been described as Sinkwich's greatest thrill at Georgia. Following the contest, a tearful Wally Butts proclaimed that the victory was the biggest thrill of his life. They both experienced additional excitement when, on the following Monday, Georgia was ranked the No. 1 team in the nation. Poschner's bewildering touchdown catch had not only stunned a packed Grant Field but placed the Bulldogs into college football's top ranking for the first time in history.

Led by Frank Sinkwich and George Poschner, Georgia earned a bid to play UCLA in the 1943 Rose Bowl. His head down, Sinkwich picks up yardage through the Bruins defense. *Photo courtesy of AP Images.*

SHIRER'S TURKEY DAY CATCH

Jimmy Shirer's key reception against Georgia Tech on Thanksgiving in 1971 leads to game-winning score

Due in large part to the play of sophomores Andy Johnson and Jimmy Poulos, newcomers on Georgia's varsity, the Bulldogs emerged from two mediocre campaigns of 1969 and 1970 as one of the nation's elite teams in 1971. Georgia was not defeated until its 10th game, against Auburn. Quarterback Johnson, much more of a runner than a passer, led a ground-oriented offense that averaged 303 rushing yards and only completed approximately five passes per game. A steadily improving Georgia Tech, the Bulldogs' final regular-season opponent, had won four games in a row, exhibiting one of college football's best defenses, in particular, against the run. The Georgia seniors had never defeated the Yellow Jackets, losing the previous two seasons by a combined 23–7 score and in the 1968 freshman game three years earlier.

What most remember about the '71 Georgia–Georgia Tech game played on Thanksgiving is a young Johnson bringing the Bulldogs down the

In his first game on Georgia's varsity, quarterback Andy Johnson runs for a first down in a 56–25 win over Oregon State. By the end of the 1971 season Johnson had already shared in several memorable Bulldogs moments, including his critical sideline-pass completion to Jimmy Shirer against Georgia Tech, which led to the Bulldogs' winning touchdown. *Photo courtesy of AP Images.*

field in the final minute and a half when they were down by three points. Georgia's acclaimed scoring and game-winning drive was capped by a one-yard dive by tailback Poulos. However, if not for the play prior to Poulos' winning plunge, the drive would have likely resulted in a tie or even a loss, instead of a 28–24 Georgia victory.

The Bulldogs trailed the Yellow Jackets by three points with 24 seconds left in the game, and Georgia was on Tech's 13-yard line with no timeouts remaining and facing second down and goal. Kicker Kim Braswell was warming up on the sideline just in case he had to attempt a game-tying field goal. Flanker Jimmy Shirer, who caught a 23-yard touchdown in the second quarter, returned to the huddle after getting "knocked out on his feet" a few plays before for the second time in the game. Johnson dropped back and threw a pass toward the right sideline. His toss was low, but Shirer made the catch, going out of bounds around the goal line. A few seconds elapsed before the referee signaled whether

Game Details

Georgia 28 • Georgia Tech 24

Date: November 25, 1971

Site: Grant Field

Attendance: 60,124

Records: Georgia 9–1; Georgia Tech 6–4

Rankings: Georgia: No. 7 (AP)/ No. 7 (UPI)

Series: Georgia 31–29–5 (Georgia Tech two-game winning streak)

> Andy Johnson can pass, in case anybody is interested.
>
> **—Vince Dooley, Georgia head coach**

ANDY JOHNSON

After leading Georgia in its 11-play, 65-yard winning drive against Georgia Tech in 1971, Andy Johnson commented to the media that it reminded him of two years prior, when he played at Athens High School. In the 1969 Georgia state championship game, senior Johnson guided the Trojans down the field for a late score and a two-point conversion to tie Valdosta High School 26-26. Johnson would direct a few other comebacks before his playing days at Georgia ended, most notably, a 35-31 victory over Tennessee as a senior.

On Georgia's freshman team in 1970, Johnson averaged 215.6 total offensive yards per game and was forecasted as college football's sophomore of the year in '71 by Playboy magazine. Labeled a "running-only" quarterback, Johnson finished the 1971 season with 870 rushing yards (second in the SEC) despite missing two games with a bruised thigh. Ironically, it was Johnson's passing (nine of 19 for 107 yards, one touchdown, no interceptions) that ultimately defeated Georgia Tech. As only a sophomore, Johnson was selected second-team All-SEC by the Associated Press.

or not Shirer scored, caught the ball in bounds short of the end zone, or caught the ball out of bounds for an incompletion. The ruling was Shirer made the catch between the 1-yard line and the goal line with 18 seconds remaining. On the next play, Poulos hurtled into the end zone for a touchdown. Tech had time for a final play, but quarterback Eddie McAshan was intercepted by Don Golden. Tears were shed by the Yellow Jackets and hearts were broken as the Bulldogs defeated their intrastate rival for the first time in three years.

Georgia, which was missing three starters because of injuries, including All-American offensive guard Royce Smith and All-SEC linebacker Chip Wisdom, had trailed Georgia Tech 14–0 and 17–7; however, the Bulldogs scratched their way back into the ballgame. Holding a 24–21 advantage, the Yellow Jackets were forced to punt from their own end zone. Tech's booming kick backed Georgia to its own 35-yard line with only 1:29 left to play.

The calm and cool Johnson promptly went to work. After throwing incomplete on first down, he was forced to run on a passing play and netted 22 yards to Georgia Tech's 43-yard line. Nevertheless, Johnson followed with three straight incomplete passes, and Georgia was confronted with fourth and 10 with 57 seconds remaining in the game. The season had come down to one play, and Johnson responded by passing on target to tight end Mike Greene over the middle for 18 yards and a critical first down. Consecutive completions to split end Lynn Hunnicutt for nine and seven yards followed, and the Bulldogs had a first and goal on the Jackets' 9-yard line with 31 seconds left. On the next snap, Johnson lost four yards and was forced to call Georgia's final timeout. On the sideline, the sophomore quarterback conferred on the next play with his coaches—a sideline pass to Shirer.

JIMMY SHIRER

Shirer was a four-sport standout at Elloree High School in Elloree, South Carolina. He was chosen all-state in football for two years, all-conference in basketball for two seasons, and a two-time state champion in track.

As a sophomore at Georgia in 1969, the one-time high school star halfback was only a backup punter, punting just one time for 42 yards. However, in 1970, Shirer caught 11 passes for 202 yards as a reserve receiver and had a 39.1 punting average as the Bulldogs' starting punter. Shirer was Georgia's most versatile player on its 11-1 and Gator Bowl champion squad of 1971. He was first on the team with 188 receiving yards on 13 catches and two touchdowns, rushed for 96 yards and a touchdown from his flanker position on 21 carries, and averaged 38.3 yards on 55 punts.

> [Shirer's catch] was the play of the game.... He made a terrific catch, and we won.
>
> **—Fred Pancoast, Georgia offensive coordinator**

Following the game, Shirer admitted he probably could have scored after making the catch but went out of bounds on purpose. He did not want to cut back in bounds after his reception and take the chance of losing yardage. Shirer said he went out of bounds because he knew Georgia could score from inside the 1-yard line on the next play. Offensive coordinator Fred Pancoast later confessed that if Shirer did not make the catch, Braswell likely would have attempted a field goal and "one of the greatest comebacks in Georgia history" would have ended, at best for the Bulldogs, in a tie game.

A REBEL-ROUSER

Herschel Walker leaps, spins, and runs over Ole Miss for six yards and a touchdown in 1981

To some Georgia fans, sophomore Herschel Walker was somewhat of a disappointment through the first four games of the 1981 season. After averaging nearly six yards per carry as a freshman and scoring 12 touchdowns in the season's final seven games, Walker was rushing for only 4.8 yards per attempt and had scored but three touchdowns. His longest run from scrimmage was just 22 yards after having seven rushes of 48 yards or more in 1980. Most importantly, Walker had lost two crucial fumbles in a 13–3 loss to Clemson—Georgia's first defeat in 16 games, dating back to 1979. Once a favorite for the Heisman Trophy, Walker was now considered only a slight possibility to win the award.

Walker was not expected to break out of his "slump" against Ole Miss. Nursing a weak ankle, Herschel had rushed for only 44 yards on 11 carries versus the Rebels as a freshman. The week of the '81 meeting with Ole Miss, he suffered a bruised foot and would be running on AstroTurf for the first time all season. Georgia had not fared

Herschel Walker dives over the pile against Ole Miss in 1981 attempting to merely gain a first down. Walker landed on the shoulders of a linebacker, spun off him and another defender, and walked into the end zone for a six-yard score. *Photo courtesy of Wingate Downs.*

HERSCHEL WALKER

Prior to playing football at Georgia, Herschel Walker had already established himself as a man of many hats. He was valedictorian of his high school senior class, an award-winning cook, a first-class runner, an excellent dancer, and a black belt in karate, to name a few interests.

The week of the Ole Miss game in 1981, Georgia practice reports never revealed how Walker actually bruised his foot. Although denied

Walker's 265 rushing yards on 41 carries against the Rebels still remain ranked third in school history for single-game accomplishments. *Photo courtesy of AP Images.*

by Walker, rumor was that he had been practicing karate kicks in the shower when he accidentally kicked a fixture. Neither an injured foot nor Steve Sloan's eight-man defensive front could stop Walker's 265-yard performance against the Rebels.

Because of his extremely outstanding three seasons at Georgia and because he might not have lived up to every expectation in the NFL, almost forgotten is Walker's exceptional career in the professional ranks. In three years with the United States Football League's New Jersey Generals (1983-1985), Walker gained 7,046 combined rushing and receiving yards, scored 61 touchdowns, and was named the league's Most Valuable Player in 1985. With Dallas, Minnesota, Philadelphia, and the New York Giants of the NFL for 12 seasons (1986-1997), Walker rushed for 8,225 yards, had 4,859 yards receiving, and 5,084 yards on kickoff returns. Unfortunately, Walker was often used as a secondary or even a blocking back during much of his time in the NFL and was on only three teams that made the playoffs. His professional career is remembered by many as not the all-time professional football (USFL and NFL combined) leader in all-purpose yardage with 25,283, but as the player dealt from Dallas to Minnesota in 1989, which ultimately yielded 19 players to the Cowboys and eventually three Super Bowl championships. Just as he is perhaps the greatest college football player ever, it can be argued that Walker is the most underappreciated professional football player in history.

well on Hemingway Stadium's turf, losing in 1975 and 1976 and winning by only a field goal in 1979.

As the game began, Ole Miss coach Steve Sloan was placing eight men on the line of scrimmage to stop Walker, and it seemed Walker's lackluster performances would continue. However, it was one rushing effort by Walker in particular, a short run at that, that jump-started his day's stellar performance and is considered perhaps his best run as a Bulldog.

Trailing 7–3, Georgia faced fourth down and inches on Ole Miss' 6-yard line midway through the second quarter. Quarterback Buck Belue turned and handed the ball to Walker, who leaped high into the air and came down around the 3-yard line for a first down. However, Walker was still on his feet as he had landed not on the ground but on the shoulders of Ole Miss' Thomas Hubbard. Walker rolled off Hubbard and another Rebel defender, maintained his balance by placing his hand on the turf, and strolled into the end zone for a touchdown.

Following an early Kevin Butler field goal, Georgia had fallen behind in the second quarter on a touchdown run by Rebel quarterback John Fourcade. Soon afterward, Fourcade left the game with injured ribs, and the Ole Miss offense would struggle from that point on.

Down by four points, the Bulldogs' offense moved from their 36-yard line to the Rebels' 6 in 13 plays. It was at this point Walker performed his acrobatic run—a leap that was designed to only gain a first down, but

Game Details

Georgia 37 • Ole Miss 7

Date: October 10, 1981

Site: Hemingway Stadium

Attendance: 41,125

Records: Georgia 3–1; Ole Miss 3–2

Rankings: Georgia: No. 11 (AP)/ No. 9 (UPI)

Series: Georgia 11-7-1 (Georgia four-game winning streak)

> [Ole Miss' defense] hit me, spun me around, and let go. I just kept running.
>
> **—Herschel Walker, tailback**

> As great a six-yard run as you will ever see. File it away in the already bulging folder of Walker's legendary runs.
>
> **—Blake Giles,** *Athens Banner-Herald* **sports editor**

Walker added a spin off of two Rebels defenders and a trot into the end zone for a head-scratching score.

After Walker's touchdown, Georgia began to throttle Ole Miss in every phase of the game. Due in large part to Walker's 150 rushing yards at halftime, the Bulldogs had a 24–7 lead at the break. Walker added 115 more in the second half before being taken out early in the final quarter of Georgia's easy 37–7 win over the Rebels.

As the final seconds ticked off the clock, Walker was paid the ultimate compliment as the opposing fans began chanting his name, not in sarcasm but in appreciation. He finished with 265 yards on 41 carries; this would be Walker's best rushing performance in his final two years at Georgia. Thrust back into the race for the Heisman Trophy, Walker had several great runs against the Ole Miss defense, including nine covering more than 10 yards and a season-long of 32. No run, however, was greater than the mere six-yarder.

SHOESTRING SINKS 'DORES

Ray Goff and Gene Washington execute the shoestring play, double-crossing the Commodores in 1975

Entering the '75 Vanderbilt meeting, Georgia had a 3–2 record for the season and had lost five of its last eight contests, including the final three games of 1974. Desperately needing a win in Nashville, the Bulldogs had sustained several key injuries, including all-conference standouts running back Glynn Harrison and offensive guard Joel Parrish.

On a wet and chilly day at Dudley Field, Georgia led the Commodores 7–3 in the second quarter. Vanderbilt's Paul Izlar lost a fumble on his own 36-yard line recovered by Georgia defensive end Lawrence Craft. On first down, quarterback Ray Goff was stopped for no gain. Suddenly, coach Vince Dooley, considered unimaginative by some for his years of running a "three yards and a cloud of dust" style of offense, became uncharacteristically innovative.

On second down, Goff approached the football, spotted on the right hash mark, as Vanderbilt stood in its defensive huddle. Goff

After taking a pitch from quarterback Ray Goff, Gene Washington, aided by a number of blocks, runs 36 yards for a touchdown, completing the "shoestring" play against Vanderbilt in 1975. *Photo courtesy of AP Images.*

RAY GOFF

Ray Goff was a star quarterback at Georgia from 1974 to 1976, alternating at the position with Matt Robinson as situations dictated. Known more as the running quarterback (Robinson the passer), Goff's 1,434 career rushing yards and 19 touchdowns are both second to Andy Johnson among quarterbacks in school history. A gifted passer as well, Goff's 136.55 career passing rating ranks ninth in school history of those completing just 10 career passes or more, trailing only Aaron Murray, Hutson Mason, D.J. Shockley, Charley Trippi, Joe Cox, David Greene, Mike Bobo, and Eric Zeier. Besides Zeier, Goff is the only Georgia

Ray Goff was perhaps the best running quarterback ever to play for Georgia. There were only a handful of occasions to cheer, however, when Goff was the Bulldogs' head coach from 1989 to 1995. *Photo courtesy of AP Images.*

quarterback to finish in the Heisman Trophy's top 10 voting, placing seventh in 1976.

Following three seasons as an assistant coach at the University of South Carolina, Goff returned to Georgia, where he held the positions of recruiting coordinator, tight ends coach, and running backs coach from 1981 to 1988. When Vince Dooley retired as Georgia's head coach, the 33-year-old Goff was surprisingly named his successor prior to the '89 season. Although an excellent recruiter, it was evident from the outset that Goff was in over his head guiding the Bulldogs. It took Goff three years before he achieved a winning season; Dooley had only one losing year in 25 campaigns. After an unsatisfactory seven-year stint, during which Georgia had only three winning campaigns and received four bowl bids, Goff was fired following the 1995 season. Since patrolling Georgia's sideline more than a decade ago, Goff has continued to live in the Athens area, where he has become a successful businessman.

knelt in front of the ball and pretended to tie his shoe as the other 10 Bulldogs nonchalantly gathered at the left hash mark on the wide side of the field. Instantly, Goff, acting as the offense's center, flipped the football to junior flanker Gene Washington. Acting as a running back, Washington raced down the left sideline with a convoy of nine blockers. Only one Commodores defender had the possibility of reaching Washington, but he was quickly blocked out of the play by split end Steve Davis. As a confused Vanderbilt defense chased to no avail, Washington easily galloped 36 yards for a touchdown with 4:58 remaining until halftime.

The Goff-to-Washington "shoestring play" jump-started a struggling squad. The Bulldogs would eventually hammer Vanderbilt 47–3 as 11 different ball carriers combined to rush for 297 yards. The Junkyard Dogs defense forced six turnovers, constantly giving Georgia's offense favorable field position.

The key to Georgia's shoestring deception was its preceding play, the 68-sweep, where Goff ran a sweep to the right hash mark. Despite not gaining any yardage, Goff's sweep set up the entire left side of the field for the Bulldogs offense to run one of the most unusual plays in football.

The play was suggested to Dooley by Georgia's offensive line coach, Jimmy Vickers, when Vickers noticed on game film that Vanderbilt's

THE SHOESTRING PLAY

On one of the most memorable and unusual plays in Bulldogs history, quarterback Ray Goff knelt on the ground pretending to tie his shoe as the Vanderbilt defense huddled nearby. Goff, acting as the offense's center, flipped the football to junior flanker Gene Washington, who raced down the left sideline. Only one Commodore had the possibility of reaching Washington, but he was quickly blocked out of the play by split end Steve Davis.

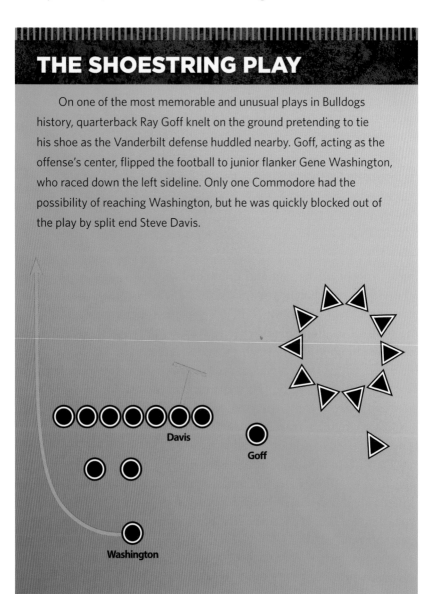

defense often held hands while calling signals in its huddle, paying little attention to the opposing offenses. In addition, Dooley was aware of the shoestring play because it was used by Duke University for a touchdown against his brother Bill's North Carolina team in 1969. Georgia ran the play three times during Thursday's practice, two days prior to the game.

The Bulldogs initially were going to attempt the chicanery on the second play of the game. However, the Georgia coaches decided to wait just a little longer to make sure the Commodore defenders would continue their inattentive huddles. The play was designed for Georgia's quarterback to lateral the ball to Harrison or Washington, but because Harrison was out with an injury, Washington, by default, would be on the receiving end of the shoestring. With little more than five minutes remaining in the second quarter, offensive coordinator Bill Pace called for the trickery, Dooley consented, and Washington executed it into the end zone as Vanderbilt's defense stood in bewilderment.

Game Details

Georgia 47 • Vanderbilt 3

Date: October 18, 1975

Site: Dudley Field

Attendance: 20,538

Records: Georgia 3-2; Vanderbilt 3-2

Series: Georgia 19-15-1 (Georgia one-game winning streak)

> The more I thought about [the shoestring play], the less I thought it would work.
>
> **—Ray Goff, quarterback**

THE DROUGHT-BREAKER

Theron Sapp's one-yard touchdown plunge ends Georgia's eight-game losing streak to the Yellow Jackets

It had seemed like forever and a day since Georgia had defeated its foremost rival, Georgia Tech. Not since 1948 had the Yellow Jackets been beaten, when John Rauch quarterbacked the Bulldogs. Rauch was now Georgia's backfield coach, nine years removed since throwing his last pass in Athens. The Bulldogs had experienced a disappointing era since their last victory over their intrastate rival: only three winning campaigns in nine seasons, just one bowl game, and a 40–49–6 overall record. However, none of the many losses were as difficult to endure as the eight in a row suffered at the hands of Georgia's hated neighbors to the southwest.

In 1957, on Georgia's ninth attempt to defeat the Jackets, the Bulldogs found themselves in a scoreless tie late in the third quarter. Georgia Tech had lost a critical fumble at midfield, and behind the running of fullback Theron Sapp, Georgia had driven to the opponent's 1-yard line. The Bulldogs were faced with fourth down and goal. Georgia had ridden the standout Sapp down the field, so there was no reason not to give him the ball in this crucial situation.

Quarterback Charley Britt gave the 196-pound junior from Macon, Georgia, the ball for the ninth time on the drive. Sapp started to his right and, aided by blocks from halfback Jimmy Orr and end Ken Cooper, found an accommodating gap and spilled over Tech's defensive line. Sapp literally fell on his face in the end zone for a touchdown. "If I hadn't stumbled on the touchdown run, I would have probably run right out the back of the end zone," Sapp said a half-century after his score.

The Bulldogs' points were their first following consecutive shutouts by Florida and Auburn and their first touchdown against Georgia Tech in four years. Most importantly, with only 2:17 remaining in the third stanza, Georgia was only a little more than a quarter away from breaking its eight-game drought to the Jackets.

Game Details

Georgia 7 • Georgia Tech 0

Date: November 30, 1957

Site: Grant Field

Attendance: 40,000

Records: Georgia 2-7; Georgia Tech 4-3-2

Series: Georgia Tech 24-22-5 (Georgia Tech eight-game winning streak)

> Eight years is a long time. All streaks always end.
>
> **—Bobby Dodd, Georgia Tech head coach**

THE GEORGIA-GEORGIA TECH RIVALRY

Only 70 miles separate the two schools whose intrastate rivalry is referred to as "clean, old-fashioned hate." Georgia and Georgia Tech have met 107 times (109 according to Tech) since 1893—the Bulldogs' second-most-played rivalry in their history. In 1919 a dispute erupted between the two schools at a baseball game followed by additional controversy during a senior parade. As a result there were no scheduled regular-season games between the teams in any sport for six years.

In the 2007 meeting of the Georgia–Georgia Tech rivalry, Yellow Jackets quarterback Taylor Bennett (No. 13) is swarmed by Georgia's Dannell Ellerbe (No. 33) and Geno Atkins during the 31–17 Bulldogs victory. The win was Georgia's seventh consecutive triumph over Georgia Tech. *Photo courtesy of AP Images.*

The two bitter rivals cannot even agree on their series record. Georgia claims to have a 64–38–5 advantage through 2007, while Georgia Tech claims two additional victories (64–40–5). Georgia discredits two losses to Tech during World War II.

The Bulldogs argue that losses in 1943 and 1944 were not to "true" Georgia Tech teams. During these seasons, the Yellow Jackets' football squad was supplemented by the V-12 Navy College Training Program, which provided former or future players from other schools.

An interesting aspect concerning the football rivalry is that the yearly winner is usually amidst a series winning streak. Georgia's victory in 2007 was its seventh consecutive win over Georgia Tech, a string that followed a Yellow Jackets three-game winning streak from 1998 to 2000, which came after seven Bulldogs wins in a row from 1991 to 1997. The longest series winning streak was when Georgia Tech was victorious for eight consecutive contests starting in 1949. The long drought was finally broken in 1957 with a 7-0 win by Theron Sapp and his fellow Bulldogs.

The game had started in 35-degree weather, and both teams seemed to feel the near-freezing effects, missing a number of scoring opportunities in the first half. On the first possession of the third quarter, Georgia Tech reached the Bulldogs' 47-yard line before losing three yards and a fumble recovered by Sapp at the midfield stripe.

From the 50-yard line, Sapp gained one yard, and halfback George Guisler followed with a five-yard rush. On third and four, Sapp bulled to the 37-yard line for a first down. Guisler rushed for only two, and Britt lost four on second down back to the Jackets' 39-yard line. Faced with an improbable conversion on third down and 12 (Georgia completed only 41 passes the entire 1957 season), Britt passed to Orr for 13 yards— the only Bulldogs completion during the entire game.

On first down, Sapp rushed for seven yards. He followed that run from the 26-yard line with consecutive rushes of three yards, seven, four, three, and one to the 1-yard line. Britt, who called every play of the game as no plays were sent in from the sideline, decided to try for the end zone himself on third down and goal but was stopped for no gain.

On fourth down, Britt elected to run a play where the fullback was to slant off tackle. The Bulldogs had attempted the same play the game before against Auburn from the 3-yard line, but they'd fumbled in the 6–0 loss. The Bulldogs would not fumble this time, however, as Sapp tumbled into the end zone for a touchdown and immortality.

> There was no way I could have not scored on fourth down and walked back to the sidelines to face my teammates.
>
> **—Theron Sapp, former Georgia fullback 50 years after his memorable touchdown**

THERON SAPP

Theron Sapp led the Bulldogs in rushing in both the 1957 and 1958 seasons. His 599 yards as a junior, including a "drought-breaking" 91 on 23 carries against Georgia Tech, were a team best since 1950. As a senior, he bettered his previous total by rushing for 635 yards and finished with 1,265 in three seasons (1956–1958) on Georgia's varsity. This total was tied for fifth-best in school history upon Sapp's graduation. As a junior, Sapp was chosen third-team Associated Press All–Southeastern Conference and, a year later, second-team AP and first-team United Press International All-SEC (Georgia's only first-team all-conference selection from 1954 to 1958).

Sapp's No. 40 jersey was retired at Georgia in 1959, joining Frank Sinkwich, Charley Trippi, and 26 years later, Herschel Walker as the only four Bulldogs to be bestowed that honor. Whereas Sinkwich, Trippi, and Walker are three of the greatest college football players of all time, Sapp, who had a fine career at Georgia and in seven seasons in the NFL, was mostly honored because of a single play he made to break the Bulldogs' longstanding drought against their despised state rival.

With approximately five minutes remaining in the game, the Yellow Jackets reached Georgia's 16-yard line before turning the ball over on downs. On the ensuing possession, Britt fumbled on his own 27-yard line, but the hero Sapp was there to recover his quarterback's blunder. The Bulldogs held on to their slim 7–0 advantage and finally defeated their arch nemesis due in large part to the effort of Sapp, forever known as "the Drought-Breaker."

CHARLEY BRITT

Charley Britt is one of the most undervalued players in Georgia football history and one of the last outstanding two-way performers. He was the Bulldogs' starting quarterback for three seasons (1957-1959), including the '59 Southeastern Conference championship squad, passing for 1,281 career yards and 11 touchdowns. A standout also on defense and returning punts, Britt tallied eight career interceptions, most notably his 100-yard return for a touchdown against Florida in 1959. Britt's commendable 11.8 career punt return average includes the 39-yard touchdown return he had to help defeat Auburn for the SEC title his senior year. In 1959 Britt was selected third-team All-SEC by the United Press International.

The 25th selection of the 1960 NFL draft, Britt played defensive back for Los Angeles, Minnesota, and San Francisco from 1960 to 1964. He made 14 career interceptions, including five in each of his first two seasons (1960 and 1961) with the Rams.

BOBO-TO-ALLEN II

Mike Bobo's touchdown pass to Corey Allen in final seconds defeats Georgia Tech for seventh consecutive season

Corey Allen told his mother not to miss the upcoming Georgia–Georgia Tech game of 1997. The Bulldogs flanker wanted to make sure that she and all their friends would be watching. The senior Allen, from Riverdale, would be returning home to Atlanta to play in his last regular-season college football game. He had played sparingly in his freshman and sophomore seasons as a Bulldog and made three starts in 1996. It was against Auburn as a junior that Allen made his unforgettable, game-tying, 30-yard touchdown reception on the final play of regulation. In his last season of 1997, Allen had finally become a starting wide receiver, and he promised his mother that he would put on a show against the Yellow Jackets.

Georgia Tech led Georgia 24–21, but the Bulldogs had moved the ball to the Jackets' 8-yard line. With only 14 seconds remaining in the game, quarterback Mike Bobo took the snap from the shotgun formation and dropped back a few steps. He lofted a fade pass toward the left corner of Tech's end zone. Bobo's pass was perfect, lobbed

Corey Allen's touchdown catch from Mike Bobo against Georgia Tech in 1997 with only eight seconds remaining was his second scoring reception in just over a year that directly led to a Georgia victory. *Photo courtesy of Getty Images.*

over Tech defensive back Travares Tillman into the waiting arms of Allen for a Georgia touchdown.

The Bulldogs now had a 27–24 advantage with only eight seconds left on the clock. The Yellow Jackets had time to run only one play. Quarterback Joe Hamilton's desperation pass fell harmlessly incomplete to the ground, and Georgia had defeated Georgia Tech for the seventh consecutive season.

Georgia had led 14–10 at halftime and sat comfortably at 21–10 following a touchdown pass from Bobo to Hines Ward late in the third quarter. However, the Yellow Jackets scored 14 consecutive points, including a three-yard touchdown run by Charles Wiley on fourth down and one and a successful two-point conversion with 48 seconds remaining in the contest.

After the Yellow Jackets' final score, giving them a three-point lead, Tech linebacker Keith Brooking warned his teammates on the sideline, "It's not over. A lot can happen in 48 ticks." It was far from over, and a lot did happen.

CHAMP BAILEY

It was soon realized that Roland "Champ" Bailey was a special football player in 1996 as he made the Southeastern Conference's all-freshman team; however, yet to be discovered was his versatility. Prior to his sophomore season, coach Jim Donnan announced that Bailey would play at wideout on offense in addition to cornerback on defense. Bailey made 12 catches in 1997, including five against Auburn. His two consecutive receptions versus Georgia Tech occurred on Georgia's game-winning drive; the first of 28 yards began the scoring possession. In Bailey's final season at Georgia in 1998, he was a star on both sides of the ball and on special teams. Champ recorded 52 tackles, three interceptions, and a team-high 744 receiving yards on 47 catches, and he appeared in a remarkable average of 87 plays per game (almost 50 on defense and slightly more than 27 on offense, and nearly 10 on special teams). The versatile, three-way standout finished seventh in the Heisman Trophy voting, the last Bulldog to appear in the top 10 of the award's balloting until linebacker Jarvis Jones in 2012.

Bailey played 15 seasons in the NFL, five in Washington and 10 with Denver. He recorded 52 career interceptions and 320 kick-/punt-return yards, made four receptions, and rushed for a touchdown in 2000.

One month after helping Georgia win a stunning victory over Florida in 1997, Champ Bailey caught two critical passes on the Bulldogs' game-winning drive against Georgia Tech. *Photo courtesy of Getty Images.*

For the third consecutive Jackets kickoff, Dave Frakes' kick went out of bounds, allowing Georgia to start its drive on the 35-yard line. On the first play, Bobo threw a slant pass to Champ Bailey, who ran all the way to Georgia Tech's 37-yard line. Bobo connected with Bailey again for seven yards and then passed to Robert Edwards for a nine-yard gain to the Jackets' 21-yard line. On first down with 21 seconds remaining, Bobo's toss over the middle was intercepted by Tillman, and the Bulldogs' chances for victory seemingly had been dashed. However, Tech's Brian Wilkins had been draped all over Ward, and fortunately for Georgia, the free safety was called for interference. The ball was placed at the 8-yard line, and the 'Dogs' rally was kept alive. On the next play, Bobo found Allen in the back corner of the end zone for the winning score.

Earlier, when it had appeared that Georgia Tech won the game after Wiley's touchdown with less than a minute left, Georgia center Brad

---

Game Details

Georgia 27 • Georgia Tech 24

Date: November 29, 1997

Site: Bobby Dodd Stadium

Attendance: 46,015

Records: Georgia 8–2; Georgia Tech 6–4

Rankings: Georgia: No. 16 (AP)/ No. 21 (ESPN)

Series: Georgia 51–33–5 (Georgia six-game winning streak)

> The Lord shined on us today and gave us another chance.
>
> **—Mike Bobo, Georgia quarterback**

Stafford reminded his teammates not to give up and "remember Auburn from last year." He was referring to the Bulldogs' come-from-behind 56–49 victory in four overtimes over Auburn the previous season after being behind 28–7 at one point. Allen certainly remembered Auburn from 1996 as he put on another show a year later against Georgia Tech for his mother, friends, and everyone else who witnessed his second game-changing, unforgettable catch.

THE FADE

In shotgun formation Mike Bobo received the snap and drifted back to the 11. Receiver Corey Allen, lined up to the left of Bobo, ran by cornerback Travares Tillman, straight into the end zone. Bobo threw a fade pass just beyond the reach of Tillman that hit Allen squarely between the numbers approximately eight yards behind the goal line for the game-winning score.

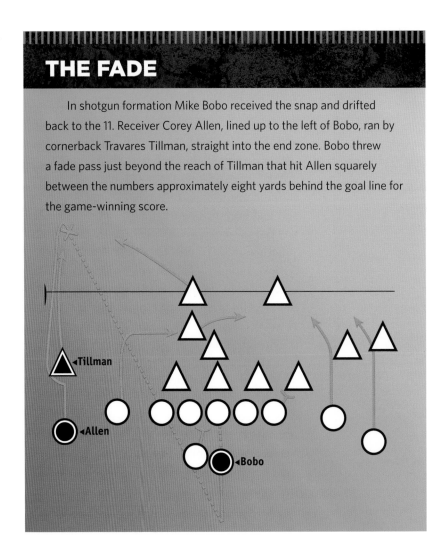

THE PERFECT BOUNCE

Fumble bounces off turf to quarterback Andy Johnson, who scoots into end zone to topple Tennessee

Underachievement and misfortune had plagued the Bulldogs during the first two months of the 1973 season. They had suffered upset losses to Vanderbilt and Kentucky and had been tied by Pittsburgh; all three teams had been 13-point underdogs or more to Georgia. Whether it was blowing a huge lead, losing a critical fumble, or throwing an interception when driving for the game-winning score, the '73 Bulldogs had experienced more than their share of bad breaks.

Entering the Tennessee game in Knoxville, Georgia had only a 3–3–1 record. With a highly probable loss pending against the Volunteers, who were a double-digit favorite, the Bulldogs were expected to have their worst start to a season after eight games since two years prior to coach Vince Dooley's arrival at Georgia.

The Bulldogs surprisingly kept the entire game close with Tennessee and were down only 31–28 late in the fourth quarter. On second down from the Volunteers' 8-yard line with a little more than one minute remaining, quarterback Andy Johnson took the snap from center. He turned and faked a handoff to fullback Bob Burns and then attempted to hand the ball to reserve tailback Glynn Harrison. Excluding participation on special teams, it was Harrison's first play of the game. In the exchange between Johnson and Harrison, the ball was dropped to Tennessee's artificial turf. Fortunately for the Bulldogs, the fumbled ball took a perfect bounce from the turf back into Johnson's hands. The alert quarterback, without hesitation, took the football on a hop and ran around his left end into the end zone for a touchdown. Georgia held off the Volunteers on their final drive and won, 35–31.

All season, the Bulldogs had struggled on offense, averaging just 259 total yards and scoring only 13 offensive touchdowns in seven games. However, against the Volunteers, Georgia seemingly ran the ball at will and matched them score-for-score early in the contest. Trailing 21–14 at halftime, Tennessee scored 17 consecutive points and led by 10 entering

Game Details

Georgia 35 • Tennessee 31

Date: November 3, 1973

Site: Neyland Stadium

Attendance: 70,812

Records: Georgia 3-3-1; Tennessee 6-1

Rankings: Tennessee: No. 11 (AP)/ No. 11 (UPI)

Series: Tennessee 8-6-2 (Tennessee two-game winning streak)

> When the ball bounced back to Andy, well, that's the way it's been bouncing [this season] for the other team.
>
> **—Jimmy Poulos, Georgia tailback**

the final quarter. The Bulldogs narrowed the gap to 31–28 following a Johnson touchdown pass with 4:27 left in the game.

The Volunteers ran three plays and were forced to punt on fourth down and two from their 28-yard line. With Tennessee's Neil Clabo set to kick, the Vols inexplicably ran a fake, snapping the ball to upback Steve Chancey. Georgia read the fake perfectly as Ric Reider and Bubba Wilson smothered Chancey for a two-yard loss.

With approximately three minutes remaining, Johnson ran for four yards on first down to Tennessee's 22-yard line. Tailback Jimmy Poulos

THE BOUNCE

Andy Johnson faked to fullback Bob Burns and tried to hand off to halfback Glynn Harrison at the 9, but the football was fumbled in the exchange. Fortunately for Georgia, the ball took a single bounce from the turf directly to Johnson. Johnson, who began running to his left after attempting his handoff, kept his momentum and, with ball in tow, ran around the left end into Tennessee's end zone for a touchdown.

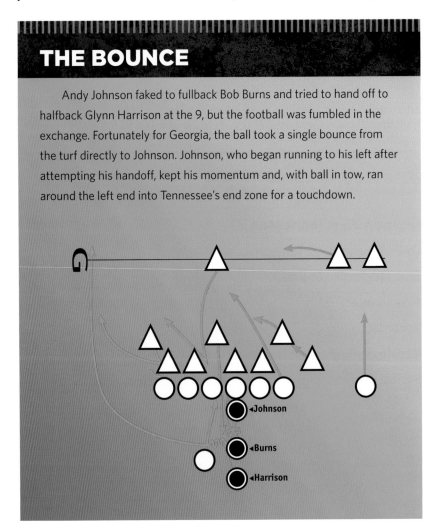

ANDY JOHNSON

Known more as a running quarterback at Georgia than as a passer, Andy Johnson rushed for 1,799 yards and passed for 1,518 from 1971 to 1973. He is the only Bulldogs quarterback in history with at least 1,000 yards passing to have more rushing yardage than passing.

Johnson appropriately did not play quarterback in the NFL but was a running back and receiver for New England from 1974 to 1981. He rushed for 2,017 career yards, caught 161 passes, and had 604 kick/punt return yards. Johnson was responsible for 26 professional touchdowns, including passing for four touchdowns in his final season on seven of nine passes for 194 yards—the only passing touchdowns, completions, and yardage for Johnson in seven NFL seasons.

carried twice to the 12 and picked up a first down. Burns followed with a four-yard run, and Georgia was faced with second and six on the Volunteers' 8-yard line.

The winning play was designed to have Harrison run up the middle, but at the last moment, Johnson pulled the football from the tailback in an attempt to keep it. The result was a fumble—a blunder that just happened to take a lucky bounce back to Johnson. If the game had been played six years earlier on Neyland Stadium's grass instead of artificial turf, the football would likely have bounced away from instead of directly to Johnson. Tennessee's Tartan Turf, the very same controversial playing surface that angered Georgia when it was installed prior to the 1968 season, had conceivably helped the Bulldogs defeat the Volunteers.

As he ran untouched toward the corner of the end zone for the game-winning touchdown, the normally emotionless Johnson branded a huge grin on his face. He and thousands of other exuberant Bulldogs could celebrate at last in 1973. Georgia had finally caught a break that had bounced from Tennessee's turf.

THIRD TIME'S A CHARM

Bob McWhorter's third attempt at the goal line finally defeats Georgia Tech

In the early years of collegiate football, the Yellow Jackets, not the Red and Black, ruled the sport in the state of Georgia. While the university often struggled to finish with a winning campaign until 1910, Georgia Tech had lost only 15 of 58 games since coach John Heisman's arrival in 1904. Heisman had defeated the Red and Black five consecutive times while at Tech. He was also 6–1–1 against Georgia as Auburn and Clemson's coach (1895–1903).

With approximately two minutes remaining in their 1910 meeting, Georgia had the ball on Tech's 4-yard line in a 6–6 tied game. The marvelous Bob McWhorter was given the ball but had difficulty crossing the Yellow Jackets' goal. On second down, he came up short again. Finally, on his third attempt, McWhorter crashed the line and scored a touchdown, giving the Red and Black an 11–6 advantage (touchdowns were worth five points from 1898 to 1911). With one and a half minutes left, the

The 1910 Georgia squad was the school's best in its first 19 seasons of playing football. The year was highlighted with an 11–6 victory over Georgia Tech. Against the Red and Black's intrastate rival, newcomer Bob McWhorter (standing, fourth from left) broke a fourth-quarter tie with a goal-line plunge late in the game. *Photo courtesy of Hargrett Rare Book & Manuscript Library/University of Georgia Libraries.*

game was called because of darkness, and Georgia had defeated Tech for the first time since 1903.

After unexpectedly beating its first five opponents of the 1910 season, Georgia was defeated by Sewanee and then fought a much-inferior Clemson team to a scoreless tie. As they had in the past, the Jackets fully expected another victory over their state rivals. Pregame comments included, "Tech will take the game," by Heisman, and "There

Along with McWhorter, coach Alex Cunningham, and John Henderson, Hafford Hay left the Gordon Institute and came to the University of Georgia in time for the 1910 football season. Hay, the Red and Black's starting quarterback in eight of the team's nine games, was considered "heady" under center and a standout on defense. Although a neophyte, it was said he ran the squad like a veteran. Despite Hay's small stature, he was also recognized as a dangerous broken-field runner.

Courtesy of www.newspaperarchive.com

In addition, Hay served as Georgia's sole kicker, converting 33 point-after touchdowns. Against Mercer, he kicked a field goal—an extremely rare occurrence for Georgia until the 1960s. Hay also tallied four touchdowns on the season, scoring a total of 56 points—second best on the squad behind McWhorter's 100.

Nothing is known regarding Hafford Hay following the Red and Blacks' successful season. He lettered only in 1910 and did not return the following year. After quarterbacking one of Georgia's greatest teams, the cool field general seemingly disappeared.

will be a Tech victory today," from Georgia Tech's generally soft-spoken captain, left end Dean Hill.

There seemed to be some validity to Hill's prophecy as Tech's captain scored the game's first points on a five-yard run in the first quarter. In the second stanza, McWhorter raced for an apparent 95-yard touchdown; however, it was "ruled his elbow out of bounds" around midfield. He was credited with a 45-yard run—one of four rushes in the contest for McWhorter gaining 25 yards or more. Nonetheless, the Georgia offense soon stalled and Tech held a 6–0 halftime lead.

Following a 30-yard punt return by George Woodruff in the final quarter, McWhorter ran around end for a 20-yard touchdown. Hafford Hay's successful conversion tied the game, and it appeared for the first time in the 13-game series that the team that scored first could lose.

On the ensuing drive, the Jackets were forced to punt despite a 40-yard penalty committed by Georgia tackle Omar Franklin for "slugging" an opposing player. Tech's defense held the Red and Black, but the Jackets' offense promptly fumbled on their own 27-yard line.

When McWhorter shot through the line to the touchdown that broke the tie, [Georgia fans] went wild, swarming down on the field.

—Dick Jemison, *Atlanta Constitution*

McWhorter ran for 23 yards to the 4-yard line before stepping out of bounds. From there, the star halfback bucked the line three times, barely scoring on his third try by three inches. Hay's point-after attempt missed, but it did not matter. In what was called "the greatest game ever," the Red and Black had finally defeated Georgia Tech, 11–6, on a short buck by Georgia's great back.

BOB MCWHORTER

Bob McWhorter came to Georgia from the Gordon Institute (a preparatory school). He instantly made an impact by scoring 12 touchdowns in the first two games of 1910. By the Georgia Tech contest, the "Gordon phenom" was already considered one of the best players in the South. McWhorter's long runs were a feature of every game, and he had a peculiar hip motion that made it difficult to tackle him after he began running.

McWhorter finished his freshman season at Georgia with 20 touchdowns. His 61 career touchdowns are unofficially a school record, while McWhorter's 331 points rank fourth (Georgia began keeping official statistics in the 1940s).

If not for insufficient documentation prior to the '40s, McWhorter would hold numerous records. In his senior season of 1913, against Alabama Presbyterian, it was reported the All-American halfback had six rushes of 50 yards or more—these runs by themselves would be sufficient for a single-game school rushing record.

Following his playing days, McWhorter, as he had been at Georgia, continued to be an authoritative figure. He earned a law degree from the University of Virginia, refereed college football games, practiced law in Athens, and served as the mayor of Athens for four terms from 1939 to 1947.

Game Details

Georgia 11 • Georgia Tech 6

Date: November 19, 1910

Site: Ponce de Leon Field

Attendance: 6,000

Records: Georgia 5-1-1; Georgia Tech 4-2

Series: Georgia Tech 6-5-1 (Georgia Tech five-game winning streak)

> Georgia's whole 11 fought like demons and snatched victory from apparent defeat by a brilliant finish.
>
> *—Athens Banner*

FRESHMAN FLOORS VOLUNTEERS

Herschel Walker runs over and through Tennessee for first touchdown as a Bulldog

Who is going to start at tailback? As Georgia approached the 1980 season, it was one of only a few questions or concerns for the Bulldogs, who were returning 18 of 22 starters from the previous year's squad that just missed winning a Southeastern Conference title and going to the Sugar Bowl. Georgia's starting tailback and leading rusher in 1979, Matt Simon, returned but was hampered with an injury. Carnie Norris had started a couple of games at tailback as a freshman in '79, and Donnie McMickens was a returning senior but had little experience. Highly recruited Herschel Walker was also vying for the starting tailback position. Although just a true freshman, even "the hostages in Iran have probably heard of Herschel Walker," wrote Billy Harper of the *Athens Banner-Herald*.

The week of Georgia's opening game it was announced that McMickens would start at tailback; Walker was the third stringer. There were concerns that Walker had played Class

Pictured as a true freshman in 1980, Herschel Walker stormed onto the college football scene by scoring two touchdowns against Tennessee in his first game. Most notable was a 16-yarder where he flattened and split the Volunteers defenders on his way into the end zone. *Photo courtesy of Getty Images.*

A high school football—the smallest classification with the smallest players. In addition, coach Vince Dooley had said Walker did not show "enough moves" in preseason practices; he would just bull over defenders instead of eluding them. Ironically, the coach would soon witness one of the greatest displays of a player bulling over and through an opposing defense.

Late in the third quarter, Tennessee held a 15–2 advantage, but Georgia had possession on the Volunteers' 16-yard line. Quarterback

THE PHENOM'S FIRST SCORE

Buck Belue took the snap and handed it to tailback Herschel Walker. Walker started to his left and immediately broke a tackle at the 15. The freshman phenom ran through a large hole and straight into the arms of safety Bill Bates at the 8. Walker literally ran over Bates, split two other approaching defenders between the 2 and 3, and sauntered over the goal line for his first of many collegiate touchdowns. "My God, a freshman!"

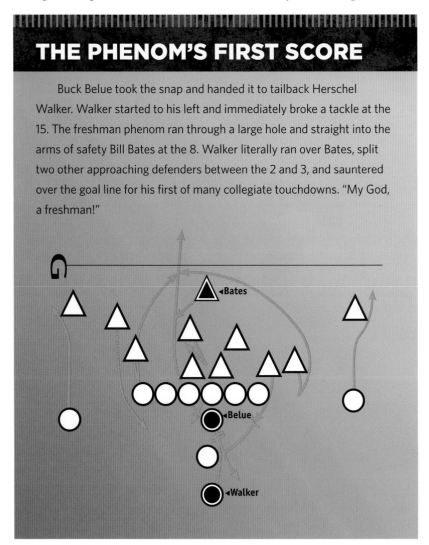

Buck Belue turned and handed the ball to Walker. The freshman started to his left, broke a tackle at the 15-yard line, and then faced safety Bill Bates, who was squared up and ready to take down the tailback. The powerful Walker ran smack into Bates at the 8-yard line. Walker's legs continued to churn as he bulled over Tennessee's safety-man. Two other Volunteers defenders converged on Walker inside the 5-yard line. Herschel split the two defensemen, leaving one, lineman Mike Casteel, lying on the turf in pain. Walker strolled the last two or so yards into the end zone for his first collegiate score—a touchdown like few had seen before and, more importantly, a scoring run that had put the Bulldogs back into the game.

In the second quarter Georgia fell behind Tennessee, 9–0, as penalties, fumbles, and missed assignments afflicted the Bulldogs. Georgia needed to ignite a stagnant offense, and Walker was inserted into the game midway through the quarter in the hope that he could provide the spark. The freshman tailback looked promising the first few times he touched the football, gaining two yards on his first carry,

Game Details

Georgia 16 • Tennessee 15

Date: September 6, 1980

Site: Neyland Stadium

Attendance: 95,288

Records: Georgia 0–0; Tennessee 0–0

Rankings: Georgia: No. 16 (AP)/ No. 20 (UPI)

Series: Tennessee 8-7-2 (Georgia one-game winning streak)

> The shortest distance between two points is a straight line.
>
> **—Herschel Walker, freshman tailback**

then rushing for six more, and later catching a pass for nine yards. Nevertheless, the Bulldogs never threatened to score and went into halftime with a nine-point deficit.

Tennessee increased its lead to 15–0 on a touchdown pass with a little more than four minutes remaining in the third quarter. The 1980 season seemed to be starting like the year prior, when Georgia began the '79 campaign with three consecutive losses. The Volunteers would be unsuccessful in their try for two points, a failing attempt that eventually cost them the game. Georgia was forced to punt on the ensuing drive. Bates caught Jim Broadway's kick at his 27-yard line and fumbled after being immediately hit by Joe Happe, who was playing with a broken hand. Georgia and Tennessee players repeatedly tried to recover Bates' miscue, and the ball traveled backward nearly 40 yards through the back of the end zone for a Georgia safety.

HERSCHEL WALKER

A full-blown recruiting war for Herschel Walker materialized among many colleges leading up to the 1980 season. Never before had an athlete been so highly recruited by the University of Georgia. There were a number of rumors, stories, and speculations regarding his college choice and why he decided Georgia over all the other pursuers. Nevertheless, the Bulldogs landed perhaps the most-prized recruit in history and took advantage of Walker's speed and power in his first game. Walker said following the victory over Tennessee, "Georgia was the best decision I ever made."

Leading up to the season opener, coach Vince Dooley remarked that he did not see Herschel making a significant contribution to the Bulldogs in '80. Walker was far from spectacular in practices and, as mentioned, entered the season as Georgia's third tailback. Even Walker admitted that he had a lot to learn. In particular, he needed to learn "more moves." However, when Georgia's offense remained sluggish against the Volunteers, Dooley inserted the freshman on "instinct." The rest is history.

After the safety and Tennessee's kickoff, the Bulldogs began the next drive at midfield. A Belue–to–Lindsay Scott pass completion for 24 yards moved the ball to the Volunteers' 16-yard line. On the next play, Walker scored his remarkable, unforgettable, and initial touchdown at Georgia.

Walker scored again with 11:16 left in the game on a nine-yard run. His second touchdown run was a lot easier than the first as he tip-toed at left end through falling defenders and ran untouched into the end zone for the score. Rex Robinson's point-after attempt was successful, and Georgia had its first lead of the night, 16–15. The Dogs barely held on to their one-point advantage, including forcing a Tennessee fumble in the final minutes at Georgia's 5-yard line.

Georgia's win over Tennessee in 1980 is memorable in many ways. Most significantly, the game introduced freshman tailback Walker—a budding superstar who, in running over Bates and into the end zone, signaled he was destined to become one of college football's best.

BILL BATES

Bill Bates, a Knoxville, Tennessee, native, was a four-year starter at safety for the University of Tennessee (1979–1982). As a junior in 1981, he led the team with four interceptions and was named Associated Press second-team All-SEC. Bates' six career fumble recoveries still rank among the best of all time at the school.

An undrafted free agent, Bates played 15 seasons as a defensive back in the NFL (1983–1997), all with the Dallas Cowboys. He and Herschel Walker were teammates for six seasons (1986–1989, 1996–1997), and both retired the same year. During his professional career, Bates recorded 18½ sacks, 14 interceptions, and seven fumble recoveries. Recognized for exceptional play on special teams, he was chosen All-Pro and went to the Pro Bowl in 1984. Bates was also a member of three Super Bowl winning teams.

CRUSHED BY A HOBNAILED BOOT

Georgia pulls upset over Vols as David Greene passes to Verron Haynes for winning score

The odds the Bulldogs faced when they traveled to play at the University of Tennessee in 2001 seemed insurmountable. Georgia, 11-point underdogs, had not won in Knoxville in 21 years and was facing a sixth-ranked Volunteers team that had defeated 38 consecutive unranked opponents in Neyland Stadium. Since 1974 the Dogs had beaten only one team as big a favorite as Tennessee (Florida in 1997). In addition, the Bulldogs' first-year coach, Mark Richt, and redshirt freshman quarterback David Greene were playing on the road for the first time. After a decade of being Tennessee's subordinate, Georgia was seeking a redefining moment with a newcomer coach and quarterback in its pursuit to become one of the conference's elite teams after years of absence.

That moment appeared to have come when it looked like the Bulldogs had won the game,

With just seconds remaining, fullback Verron Haynes catches a six-yard touchdown pass from David Greene to defeat Tennessee in 2001. *Photo courtesy of AP Images.*

LARRY MUNSON

Larry Munson was the legendary voice of the Dogs as Georgia football's play-by-play announcer from 1966 to 2008. Munson's broadcasting career, which exceeded six decades, began with calling University of Wyoming football games in the 1940s. Known, among other names, as "the 12th Man" of Bulldogs football, Munson's one-of-a-kind, emotion-filled, gravely voice was considered one of the very best in all of sports.

Munson was just as much a part of Georgia football lore as Herschel Walker, Vince Dooley, or mascot Uga. One of his greatest calls was against Tennessee in 2001, when, following Verron Haynes' winning score, Munson blurted, "We just stepped on their face with a hobnailed boot and broke their nose. We just crushed their face."

Prior to the start of the 2007 season, after 41 years, the 84-year-old Munson announced he would only broadcast home games because of his failing health. He stepped down early in the 2008 season, and passed away on November 20, 2011.

For more than four decades, Larry Munson was the voice of Georgia Bulldogs football. Many of his calls are legendary, including his "hobnailed boot" call when David Greene connected with Verron Haynes to defeat Tennessee. *Photo courtesy of AP Images.*

but then victory seemed to be snatched from the Bulldogs with under a minute remaining. However, led by the direction of freshman Greene, Georgia placed itself in a position for another opportunity to achieve a major upset.

With only 10 seconds left to play, the Bulldogs lined up in a three-receiver set, facing first down and goal on Tennessee's 6-yard line and trailing 24–20. On a play called P-44-Haynes, Greene ran a play-action pass, faking a handoff to the tailback. Meanwhile, fullback Verron Haynes feigned a block on blitzing middle linebacker Dominique Stevenson and slipped unseen into the end zone. Stevenson bit on Greene's play-action, leaving no defender within five yards of Haynes. Greene calmly floated a soft pass to the wide-open fullback for a touchdown. Georgia had retaken the lead, 26–24, and would be only five seconds from accomplishing a stunning victory.

Game Details

Georgia 26 • Tennessee 24

Date: October 6, 2001

Site: Neyland Stadium

Attendance: 107,592

Records: Georgia 2-1; Tennessee 3-0

Rankings: Tennessee: No. 6 (AP)/ No. 7 (ESPN)

Series: Tennessee 17-11-2 (Georgia one-game winning streak)

> By the grace of God I caught the ball. That was the longest five seconds, but the ball finally got there.
>
> **—Verron Haynes, Georgia fullback**

With 5:44 left in the game, a field goal by Georgia's Billy Bennett had broken a 17–17 tie. A Bulldogs win appeared certain when Jermaine Phillips intercepted Tennessee's Casey Clausen with 1:53 remaining. Georgia's offense then ran three plays and was forced to punt. Four plays later, from his own 38-yard line, Clausen threw a short screen pass to Travis Stephens, who raced down his left sideline for a 62-yard touchdown with only 44 seconds remaining in the contest. Stephens

VERRON HAYNES

A transfer from Western Kentucky University to Georgia before the 1999 season, Verron Haynes was a seldom-used blocking back prior to the 2001 Tennessee game. Following the win over Arkansas the week before, Haynes demanded of coach Mark Richt to "give me the ball." Richt obliged.

Against the Volunteers, Haynes caught four passes for 59 yards, including the game-winning touchdown. Two weeks later against Kentucky, he rushed for 86 yards, caught three passes for 73 yards, and scored three touchdowns. By the end of the season, with Musa Smith hampered with injuries and Jasper Sanks kicked off the team, Haynes had been switched from fullback to tailback and was Georgia's primary running threat. In the Bulldogs' final four games, including the Music City Bowl against Boston College, Haynes averaged more than 163 rushing yards on 29 carries per game and scored a total of five touchdowns. His 691 rushing yards, not including 132 in the Music City Bowl, led the team in 2001. Haynes' best rushing performance was 207 yards on 39 carries against Georgia Tech. Through the 2014 season, he is only one of 10 Bulldogs (along with Charles "Rabbit" Smith, Charley Trippi, Kevin McLee, Herschel Walker, Lars Tate, Rodney Hampton, Garrison Hearst, Todd Gurley, and Nick Chubb) to rush for 200 or more yards in a single game since 1945.

In 68 career games in the NFL, he rushed for 738 yards, caught 61 passes, and scored five touchdowns.

and the Volunteers had presumably broken the Bulldogs' hearts and regained the lead, 24–20.

Tennessee's plan to not give Georgia good field position on the ensuing kickoff by squib-kicking backfired, as Randy McMichael took the squib at his own 34-yard line and returned it seven yards. As Greene huddled with his offense, the young but poised quarterback told them they "gotta believe," stay focused, and they had plenty of time to score. On first down, Greene passed short to Damien Gary, who avoided a tackle and gained 13 yards to Tennessee's 46-yard line. With 34 seconds remaining, Greene threw incomplete to Michael Johnson, but on second down, Greene threw a 26-yard gain to McMichael, running a seam route and making a one-handed diving catch of a pass that was nearly intercepted. With 20 seconds left to play from the 20-yard line, Greene found McMichael again for 14 yards with a defensive back draped all over him. The Bulldogs called their final timeout to set up P-44-Haynes.

In four games at Georgia, Richt had almost called the play on several occasions but waited until the perfect opportunity arose. In the huddle, Haynes said he was surprised when the play was called and said a quick prayer before lining up at fullback. At the line of scrimmage, Greene's assignment was to check Tennessee's defensive alignment. If the Volunteers had one safety positioned, the quarterback was instructed to throw the ball away. If two safeties were present, the play should work to perfection. Tennessee's defensive formation included two safeties, and Haynes' prayer was answered.

END AROUND TO APPLEBY

Tight end Richard Appleby runs from left to right, plants his feet, and throws an 80-yard bomb to defeat Florida

The Bulldogs of the mid-1970s won ballgames with a tenacious and attacking Junkyard Dogs defense and a consistent and skilled running game. In the 1975 Florida game, neither Georgia's offense nor its defense was particularly effective.

As the No. 11 Gators had done for most of the season, they were in total control against the Bulldogs but only led 7–3 with less than four minutes remaining in the contest. For any chance of victory in the final minutes, Georgia would need to resort to something other than running the football and then hope the Junkyard Dogs could hold down the second-best offense in the nation.

On a wet Gator Bowl surface late in the game, Florida drove to Georgia's 38-yard line with a four-point lead but was forced to punt. Tom Dolfi's kick went into the end zone and was brought out to Georgia's 20-yard line. On first down, quarterback Matt Robinson took the snap and faced his left. Senior Richard Appleby, as he had done several times during the season, ran

The 1975 Georgia-Florida game was far from over even when the Bulldogs scored on the Richard Appleby-to-Gene Washington 80-yard pass. The Gators had two additional possessions, and it was up to defensive coordinator Erk Russell's (pictured) Junkyard Dogs to keep Florida off the scoreboard. *Photo courtesy of Hargrett Rare Book & Manuscript Library/University of Georgia Libraries.*

an end around from his left to right and was handed the football by Robinson. From his tight end position, Appleby carried the football six times in 1975, but on this particular play, he would suddenly stop and plant his feet on the rain-soaked turf. Appleby arched back his right arm and threw a long, wobbly spiral nearly 50 yards in the air. Flanker Gene Washington, left all alone by an unsuspecting Gators secondary, caught the ball in stride around Florida's 35-yard line and easily strolled untouched into the end zone for a touchdown, waving the football in the air in celebration. Georgia had struck quickly on a trick passing play and had assumed its first lead over the Gators with 3:12 left in the game.

Nonetheless, the 54th Georgia-Florida meeting was far from over. Trailing 10–7, the Gators reached the Bulldogs' 36-yard line before quarterback Don Gaffney was sacked by defensive end Dicky Clark, resulting in a fumble recovered by cornerback David Schwak. Georgia was forced to punt, and the Gators flew down the field again and had a first and 10 on the Bulldogs' 21-yard line. Gaffney proceeded to throw three consecutive incomplete passes. With just 50 seconds remaining, Florida kicker David Posey lined up to attempt a game-tying, 38-yard field goal. His kick was unsuccessful, barely getting off the ground, and Georgia had upset the Gators.

The Appleby-to-Washington end around, or wide-counter pass, had been called by offensive coordinator Bill Pace at halftime. The play was set up throughout the game as Georgia executed four end-around runs (two each by Appleby and Washington), netting 38 yards and three first downs. The Bulldogs figured another end-around play would

Game Details

Georgia 10 • Florida 7

Date: November 8, 1975

Site: Gator Bowl

Attendance: 70,416

Records: Georgia 6–2; Florida 7–1

Rankings: Florida: No. 11 (AP)/ No. 10 (UPI)

Series: Georgia 32–19–2 (Georgia one-game winning streak)

> I had been throwing it well in practice. I saw Gino [Washington] wide open; I knew it was a TD.
>
> **—Richard Appleby, tight end**

MATT ROBINSON

Georgia's second-string quarterback heading into the 1974 season, Matt Robinson quickly claimed the starting position and was one of the few Bulldogs bright spots during a 6–6 campaign. Robinson directed an offense that finished second in the conference (397.7 yards per game), while his 1,317 passing yards were a Southeastern Conference best. He also rushed for 265 yards and seven touchdowns. With the start of the 1975 season, Georgia moved to more of a run-oriented offense. Robinson split time with running quarterback Ray Goff, passing for only 978 combined yards in 1975 and 1976. Robinson, recognized as a knowledgeable and intelligent quarterback and a perfect fit in Georgia's veer offense, completed his collegiate career by directing the Bulldogs, along with Goff, to an SEC title in 1976.

Robinson was a ninth-round selection of the New York Jets in the 1977 NFL draft. Primarily a backup from 1977 to 1982 with New York, Denver, and Buffalo, Robinson left for the Jacksonville Bulls of the United States Football League in 1984 and played for Portland the following season.

After retiring from professional football, Robinson has worked as an assistant coach at a number of area high schools and remains a successful businessman.

catch Florida off guard. To throw against the Gators' excellent pass defense, Georgia would have to use trickery as Ray Goff and Robinson had combined to complete just two of nine passes for 29 yards and two interceptions in the game.

When Appleby received the handoff from Robinson, he waited patiently for Florida's secondary to pull up from pass coverage and play the run. Once they did, Appleby stopped and flung the ball to a streaking Washington, who had run by cornerback Harry Davis. As Washington ran by Davis, the Gators defender attempted to knock down the Bulldogs

THE END AROUND

Matt Robinson faced his left and faked a handoff to running back Glynn Harrison. Tight end Richard Appleby, who had lined up to Robinson's left, came off the line and was handed the ball by the quarterback. Appleby ran to the right, waiting for Florida's secondary to defend Georgia's apparent running play. At the 12 Appleby suddenly stopped and threw a bomb to a waiting Gene Washington. Washington caught the pass in stride at the Gators' 35 and coasted into the end zone untouched.

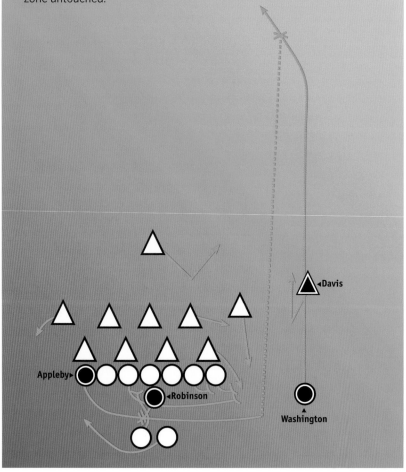

speedster but to no avail. Seconds later, Washington and his teammates were celebrating in the end zone, having completed the 80-yard play.

Following the 10–7 Georgia victory, Appleby commented that the end-around play was only his third pass attempt while playing organized football. This one against Florida had far better results than his previous two: an interception thrown while playing for Clarke Central High School in Athens, Georgia, and a second interception thrown only three weeks prior against Vanderbilt.

Washington, who made several big plays during his career at Georgia, said that his end-around catch from Appleby was "the biggest. It has to be."

RICHARD APPLEBY

Along with Horace King, Larry West, Chuck Kinnebrew, and Clarence Pope in 1971, Richard Appleby was in the first group of African American football recruits at the University of Georgia. Because freshmen were not eligible to play until 1972 and because of academic problems, Appleby did not see varsity action until 1973. However, once he finally stepped foot on the field, Appleby was a permanent fixture for the Bulldogs, starting three seasons (1973–1975) at tight end. Appleby started the last half of the '73 season at split end, filling in for an injured Gene Washington.

Appleby was only the second Bulldog ever to lead Georgia in receiving three separate seasons. Appleby's 902 career receiving yards was seventh all time upon his departure from the school. His 18.8 career receiving average is fourth best for players with 45 career catches or more. Appleby also rushed seven times for 68 yards while at Georgia and completed one pass for 80 yards—the end-around touchdown against Florida in '75.

A fourth-round selection by Tampa Bay in the 1976 NFL draft, Appleby never played a down of professional football. Today, he is a successful businessman in Hawaii.

B-E-L-U-E SPELLS RELIEF

Freshman Buck Belue comes off bench against Yellow Jackets and tosses game-winning touchdown on fourth down

The Wonderdogs of 1978, picked in the preseason to finish eighth or lower in the Southeastern Conference, continued to surprise everyone as they were instead ranked eighth in the nation with an 8-1-1 record entering the Georgia Tech game. A Sugar Bowl berth and a conference championship were still very much a possibility for the "Cardiac Kids," who had rallied for victories in five games, including deficits of 14-0 and 16-0 to Louisiana State and Kentucky, respectively.

The Dogs would need another successful comeback effort to defeat the Yellow Jackets, and they were down 20-0 midway through the second quarter. Things had gotten so bad that quarterback Jeff Pyburn was benched with 4:38 until halftime in favor of freshman Buck Belue.

Belue did rally Georgia, but Georgia Tech still held a 28-21 advantage late in the game. The Bulldogs faced fourth down and three on the

Yellow Jackets' 42-yard line with fewer than three minutes remaining. Belue took the snap and rolled to his right. He thought about running for the first down until two Tech defenders grabbed a hold of him. Belue broke containment and suddenly spotted receiver Amp Arnold, who had slipped past a cornerback to become wide open. The freshman quarterback lofted a pass to a waving Arnold, who caught it near the Yellow Jackets' 20-yard line and ran easily and untouched into the end zone. Georgia would go on to win 29–28. Belue's celebrated pass would be his greatest as a Bulldog until nearly two years later in Jacksonville against the Florida Gators.

Two Willie McClendon touchdown runs cut Georgia's deficit to 20–14 in the third quarter. The Bulldogs scored their third consecutive

Freshman quarterback Buck Belue sits on the sideline after his fourth-down touchdown pass to Amp Arnold and subsequent two-point conversion defeated Georgia Tech in 1978. *Photo courtesy of Hargrett Rare Book & Manuscript Library/University of Georgia Libraries.*

WILLIE McCLENDON

Despite being Georgia's primary running back for only one season, Willie McClendon finished his career as the school's third all-time leading rusher with 2,228 yards and still remains ranked 10th after more than 35 years. Playing behind Kevin McLee, McClendon combined to rush for more than 900 yards in 1976 and 1977. As a senior in 1978 and getting the majority of the carries at Georgia's tailback position, McClendon rushed for 1,312 yards, including 100 or more in each of the Bulldogs' first eight games of the season.

A third-round NFL selection in 1979 by Chicago, McClendon spent four years with the Bears (1979–1982), backing up the great Walter Payton. Following a three-year playing career in the United States Football League, McClendon was an assistant coach at Valdosta State College for three seasons. He returned to Athens in 1989 to become Georgia's running backs coach for the first five years of the Ray Goff regime (1989–1993), coaching the likes of Rodney Hampton, Larry Ware, Garrison Hearst, Mack Strong, and Terrell Davis.

Willie's son Bryan was a receiver at Georgia from 2002 to 2005, catching 56 career passes for 830 yards. Bryan currently serves as Georgia's wide receivers coach.

Losing 20–0 in the second quarter against the Yellow Jackets, Willie McClendon's two touchdown runs put the Bulldogs back into the game. The All-SEC tailback began the 1978 season with eight consecutive 100-yard rushing performances. *Photo courtesy of Hargrett Rare Book & Manuscript Library/University of Georgia Libraries.*

touchdown on an electrifying punt return by Scott Woerner, and Georgia led for the first time. However, on the ensuing kickoff, Georgia Tech's Drew Hill returned the kick from behind his own goal line and went more than 100 yards for a score. The Yellow Jackets had jumped back ahead, 28–21, late in the third quarter.

Following a Georgia Tech punt, Georgia had possession on its own 16-yard line with 5:52 remaining in the game. After three plays, the Bulldogs faced fourth and two on the 24. Belue rolled out for a six-yard gain and a critical first down. On the next play, Arnold, a high school quarterback, completed a 21-yard pass to tailback Matt Simon. The following three plays netted Georgia seven yards, and the Wonderdogs were faced with their second fourth-down play of the drive.

The acclaimed touchdown pass was only supposed to be a quick-out reception for a five- to six-yard gain. Belue could not throw the quick-out because Arnold was covered, so he decided to run upfield. As soon as Belue began to run, Arnold's defender decided to run toward

Game Details

Georgia 29 • Georgia Tech 28

Date: December 2, 1978

Site: Sanford Stadium

Attendance: 59,700

Records: Georgia 8-1-1; Georgia Tech 7-3

Rankings: Georgia: No. 11 (AP)/ No. 8 (UPI)

Series: Georgia 36–29–5 (Georgia Tech one-game winning streak)

> I didn't see [Arnold] catch it, but I jumped off the ground to see him score.
>
> **—Buck Belue, quarterback**

the quarterback to assist with the tackling, leaving Arnold wide open. After Belue avoided being tackled, he spotted Arnold all alone, threw him the ball, and Arnold scored with 2:24 left on the clock.

Two weeks earlier, Georgia had decided to kick a point-after touchdown late in its game to tie Auburn, 22–22. The tie would

THE FOURTH-DOWN FORTUNE

Freshman Buck Belue took the snap and immediately began sprinting to his right, looking to throw. For an instant, he decided to turn upfield and run for a first down. Unexpectedly Belue spotted a wide-open Amp Arnold. Arnold had initially executed a quick-out route, but as soon as Belue began to run, the receiver continued his pass pattern downfield. As he was being grabbed, and just before getting brought down, Belue decided against running and instead tossed a pass to Arnold. Arnold caught the football on the 23 and sprinted across the Yellow Jackets' goal line.

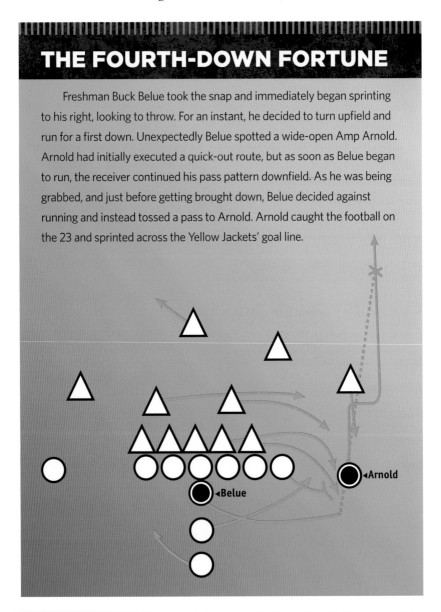

eventually cost the Bulldogs an SEC title. Down 28–27 to Georgia Tech, they decided to try for the two-point conversion and the win. Belue first threw incomplete, but pass interference was ruled on the Yellow Jackets. Given a second chance, Belue faked to McClendon, kept to his left, and pitched the ball to Arnold, who strolled across the goal line for the two-point score.

On their final drive, the Yellow Jackets moved from their 9-yard line to Georgia's 37. However, Tech's Mike Kelley was intercepted by David Archer, another Bulldogs star freshman of the game. The interception preserved Georgia's 29–28 victory. Nonetheless, the comeback victory is most remembered for the fourth-down scoring pass thrown by an unproven newcomer in rallying Georgia past its state rival.

BUCK BELUE

A highly recruited football and baseball player from Valdosta, Georgia, Belue's distinguished collegiate football career first garnered attention when he rallied the Bulldogs past Georgia Tech in '78. As he had against the Yellow Jackets, Belue supplanted Jeff Pyburn as the starting quarterback in 1979 and rallied Georgia to a 6–5 record and nearly an SEC title and Sugar Bowl birth after an 0–3 start. Belue is the only Georgia quarterback to lead the Bulldogs to successive conference titles (1980-1981) and an undisputed national championship (1980). His 90.0 winning percentage (27-3 record) as a starting quarterback is a school record and upon graduation ranked second-best of all time in college football behind Nebraska's Jerry Tagge's, who achieved 94.2 percent (24-1-1).

Belue participated in both professional baseball and football. He played three years in the Montreal Expos' farm system and was the third-leading passer of the United States Football League's Jacksonville Bulls in 1985. He later was a coach at Valdosta State University and a TV sports anchor in Savannah, Georgia. Belue currently cohosts an afternoon radio sports talk show in Atlanta.

GEORGIA'S FAMOUS FLEA-FLICKER

Moore-to-Hodgson-to-Taylor covers 73 yards and shocks national champion Alabama

The Bulldogs faced the daunting task of opening the 1965 season against Bear Bryant's Alabama Crimson Tide. Alabama, college football's winningest team of the 1960s, was in the seventh season of nine consecutive in which it would finish in the final Associated Press top-10 rankings. The Crimson Tide was declared the national champion in 1964 by the two major polls, the AP and United Press International, and had defeated Georgia five straight seasons by an average scoring margin of nearly four touchdowns per victory.

Georgia, on the other hand, was just starting to turn its football program around. After 15 years of mostly inadequate play, the Bulldogs began a new era in 1964 under the leadership of newly hired coach Vince Dooley. Dooley guided his first Georgia team to seven wins and a Sun Bowl victory—only the Bulldogs' second bowl

Preston Ridlehuber (No. 12) helps an exhausted Pat Hodgson (No. 87) off the field following Georgia's flea-flicker play in 1965 against Alabama. Hodgson began the 73-yard play by first catching a short pass from Kirby Moore. *Photo courtesy of Hargrett Rare Book & Manuscript Library/University of Georgia Libraries.*

appearance in 14 seasons. Although the 51st meeting between the schools was being played in Athens, a Georgia win appeared highly unlikely. It seemed a miracle would need to occur for the Bulldogs to claim a victory over the Tide—a miracle that indeed transpired.

After leading 10–0 in the second quarter, Georgia allowed Alabama to score 17 consecutive points, including a short scoring run by quarterback Steve Sloan with only 3:14 left in the game. On the ensuing possession, Georgia had the ball on its own 27-yard line, trailing by seven points. Dating back to the previous season, the Bulldogs had scored only three offensive touchdowns in their last four games, and there was no reason to believe they could mount a scoring drive against Alabama's mighty defense. It would likely take some sort of freakish play for any success, so Dooley reached into his bag of tricks.

Kirby Moore took the snap from center Ken Davis and rolled slightly to his left. As Alabama's Tom Somerville closed in on the quarterback,

Game Details

Georgia 18 • Alabama 17

Date: September 18, 1965

Site: Sanford Stadium

Attendance: 41,500

Records: Georgia 0-0; Alabama 0-0

Rankings: Alabama: No. 5 (AP)

Series: Alabama 28-18-4 (Alabama five-game winning streak)

> The Bulldogs executed a blackboard dandy just like coach Vince Dooley diagrammed it.
>
> **—Harry Mehre, former Georgia head coach (1928-1937)**

Moore threw and completed a short pass to end Pat Hodgson at the 37-yard line. Just as Hodgson began to drop to a knee, he smoothly lateraled the ball to the left of Alabama's Frank Canterbury into the hands of trailing teammate Bob Taylor. Taylor outsped linebacker Paul Crane to the sideline and took off down the left side, completing a 73-yard flea-flicker touchdown play with 2:08 remaining in the ballgame and Georgia trailing by a single point.

Following the flea-flicker play and down 17–16 to the Crimson Tide, Georgia elected to try a two-point conversion as quarterback Kirby Moore (bottom left, No. 14) rolls out to his right looking for a receiver. *Photo courtesy of Hargrett Rare Book & Manuscript Library/University of Georgia Libraries.*

What many Bulldogs fans are unaware of is that more drama unfolded in the contest's final two minutes—drama that is the reason why Georgia's famous flea-flicker play is ranked seventh of all time instead of in the top three.

After the touchdown, Dooley called back kicker Bob Etter to return to the sideline; Georgia was going for two points and the lead instead of kicking the extra point for a tie. Moore completed his second short pass to Hodgson in two plays, and the Bulldogs took an 18–17 advantage.

Following the kickoff, Alabama had great field position on its own 41-yard line. Quickly, the Crimson Tide moved to Georgia's 26 with 14 seconds left on the clock. In a bid to reclaim the lead and a victory that seemed lost, Alabama kicker David Ray lined up to attempt a 42-yard, game-winning field goal. Ray's kick fell short and wide left, and Georgia

BOB TAYLOR

"Bullet" Bob Taylor came to Georgia in 1962 without a scholarship but departed in 1965 as the school's 11th all-time leading rusher. He finished his sophomore season as the Bulldogs' first-team left halfback and was second on the team in both rushing and scoring. On Vince Dooley's first Georgia team in 1964, Taylor was second on the team in rushing and kickoff returns and was considered an all-SEC contender for his upcoming senior year.

In 1965 he was recognized as "one of the greatest runners in Georgia history" as he tallied 321 rushing yards and a 4.9 average (for the season, the team, as a whole, averaged 3.2 yards per carry) in just five games. In the Bulldogs' fifth contest of the year, Taylor had rushed for 69 yards on 12 carries against Florida State. With three minutes remaining in the third quarter, Georgia had a 3–0 lead when Taylor exited the game with a broken leg. The Bulldogs would eventually lose 10–3, and Taylor would never play football again.

Taylor practiced law in LaGrange, Georgia, before retiring from the profession. He passed away on August 7, 2014, at his home in LaGrange.

regained possession. Moore needed to only run a quarterback sneak to finish off the highly favored Crimson Tide and give Coach Dooley one of the most significant victories in Georgia football history.

The flea-flicker play had been put in Georgia's practice regimen the week of the Alabama game after Dooley, a former Auburn assistant coach, remembered it was previously used by Georgia Tech against the Tigers. Dooley called the play at the perfect time,

Coaches Paul "Bear" Bryant (left) and Vince Dooley (right) meet at midfield following Georgia's shocking 18-17 win over Alabama. *Photo courtesy of Hargrett Rare Book & Manuscript Library/University of Georgia Libraries.*

THE FLEA-FLICKER

Kirby Moore rolled out, and just before Alabama's Tom Somerville reached him, fired a short pass to end Pat Hodgson at the 37. Dropping to a knee and surrounded by defenders, Hodgson lateraled the ball backward to Bob Taylor, who had been trailing Moore's pass. Catching the lateral at the 33, Taylor ran toward the left sideline and was soon in the clear, easily outdistancing the Crimson Tide defenders for a long touchdown.

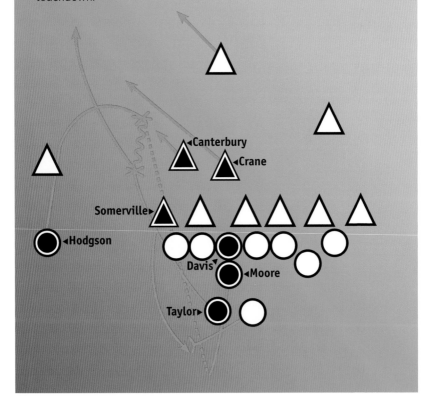

following Sloan's apparent game-clinching touchdown and as many Bulldogs fans were leaving Sanford Stadium, conceding a loss. And although people even today question whether Hodgson had control of the football before he lateraled to Taylor, which would have negated Taylor's touchdown, the flea-flicker ultimately defeated the seemingly invincible Crimson Tide.

KIRBY MOORE

Kirby Moore was Georgia's number one quarterback on its 1963 freshman team. While playing on the Bulldogs' B-team the following season, Moore nearly quit the squad to play baseball exclusively. However, when he realized how well he performed against Georgia's varsity defense in practice, Moore decided to continue playing football. In Georgia's '65 season opener against Alabama, the sophomore came off the bench to relieve senior starter Preston Ridlehuber, who was injured with pulled muscles. Moore rushed for 43 yards and passed for 99, including 73 yards on the winning flea-flicker play.

Because of Moore's presence, Ridlehuber was eventually moved to halfback. Moore would be Georgia's chief signal-caller from 1965 to 1967. He was only the fourth Bulldog, joining John Rauch, Zeke Bratkowski, and Larry Rakestraw, to lead Georgia in passing for three seasons since 1940. A fantastic running-passing combination quarterback, Moore is second of all Georgia quarterbacks in career passing yardage (1,710), who have in addition rushed for 1,000 or more yards, trailing only James Jackson (1984–1987). Statistics aside, the highlight of Moore's career at Georgia was leading the Bulldogs to a 10-1 record and Southeastern Conference title as a junior in 1966.

Currently, Moore heads the law firm Kirby R. Moore, LLC, in Macon, Georgia.

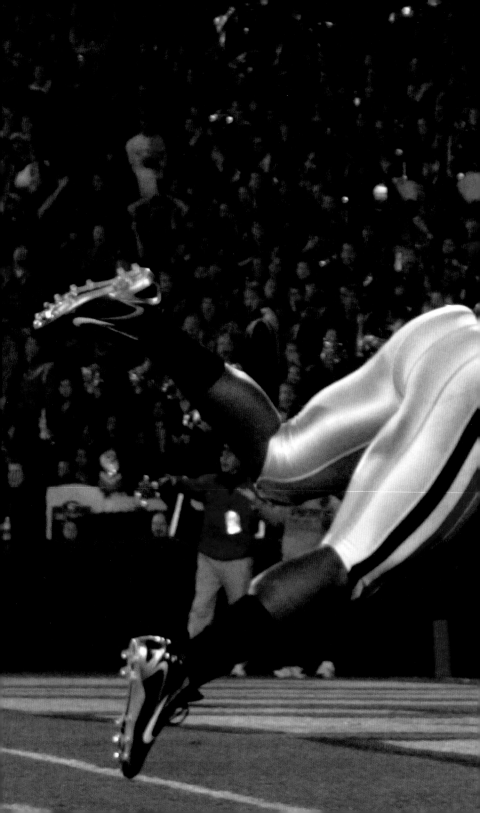

THE BEST OFFENSE IS A GOOD DEFENSE

GREAT SCOTT!

Jake Scott intercepts Kentucky in '68 and twists and whirls his way to a touchdown

Despite having only a subpar record, the '68 Kentucky Wildcats were called "the best 2–3 football team in America" by their head coach, Charlie Bradshaw. The football team was perhaps the school's best since the Bear Bryant–coached Wildcats bowl squads of the early 1950s. For the Georgia game, however, Kentucky's starting quarterback, Stan Fortson, would not be able to play because of appendicitis. Backup Dave Bair, who led the SEC in 1967 with 21 interceptions thrown, would be filling in for Fortson and facing a Bulldogs defense ranked second in the conference, on a chilly night in Lexington, Kentucky.

Georgia had one of the nation's best defenses and, in the opinion of many, the very best safety-man in all of college football in Jake Scott. Scott displayed his excellence against the Wildcats with two interceptions returned for touchdowns; the second return was especially praiseworthy.

With the Bulldogs holding a two-touchdown lead in the final quarter, Scott intercepted a pass by Bair intended for all-purpose star Dicky Lyons

Following his interception against Kentucky in 1968, it appeared that Jake Scott would be tackled. However, the junior safety-man escaped from his would-be tackler and ran 35 yards for a touchdown. *Photo courtesy of AP Images.*

at the Kentucky 35-yard line. Scott was hemmed in and trapped by Lyons, and it appeared that Scott was soon to be tackled. However, the All-American safety planted his feet, completely turned around, and left a falling Lyons grasping for air. Scott dashed down the right sideline on an unbelievable return for a score.

Jake Scott (No. 13) attempts to break a tackle in the 1969 Sugar Bowl, his final game as a Bulldog. Scott ended his college career with 16 interceptions in only two seasons, which remains the school record. *Photo courtesy of AP Images.*

Scott scored the first points of the game on an interception return with 3:49 remaining in the first quarter. Defensive tackle Bill Stanfill deflected a Bair pass into Scott's arms, who then returned the deflection 33 yards for a touchdown.

Georgia led Kentucky 21–0 at halftime. The Bulldogs defense dominated the 'Cats in the first two quarters of play, yielding no first downs and only 32 total yards.

With just under eight minutes left in the game, Kentucky trailed 21–7 and had the ball on its own 17-yard line. Bair's pass was intercepted by Scott, and for the second time, Georgia's standout safety returned the ball for a touchdown on, according to writer Furman Bisher, "an even more special run [than Scott's first return]." For the game, Scott led a Georgia defense that allowed the Wildcats to score only in the final quarter in a 35–14 win.

Game Details

Georgia 35 • Kentucky 14

Date: October 26, 1968

Site: Stoll Field/McLean Stadium

Attendance: 32,000

Records: Georgia 4-0-1; Kentucky 2-3

Rankings: Georgia: No. 8 (AP)/No. 8 (UPI)

Series: Georgia 14-5-2 (Georgia two-game winning streak)

> You don't ever think you're going to score [after making an interception]. You just run where there ain't nobody.
>
> **—Jake Scott, safety**

JAKE SCOTT

As one of only two sophomore starters, along with left guard Steve Greer, on Georgia's 1967 defense, Jake Scott demonstrated an outstanding ability to both defend the pass and return punts. He would soon display his knack for returning interceptions and punts for touchdowns.

Against Florida in '67, the varsity newcomer returned a Gator interception 32 yards for a score. Prior to Scott's two touchdown returns against Kentucky in 1968, Scott's final year at Georgia, he took a Tennessee punt back 90 yards for a score, although in the process he endured three hits by would-be Volunteers tacklers. In 1970, as a rookie for the Miami Dolphins, Scott returned a punt 77 yards for a touchdown in a 34–17 win over Baltimore.

Following only two years at Georgia and a stellar nine-season career in the NFL, Scott, for personal and unacknowledged reasons, disassociated himself from Georgia football until he acted as the Bulldogs' honorary captain for a 2006 game against Georgia Tech.

Besides defending the pass, Jake Scott was also an excellent punt returner. Here he returns a Tennessee punt 90 yards for a touchdown in the season-opening game of 1968. *Photo courtesy of Hargrett Rare Book & Manuscript Library/ University of Georgia Libraries.*

To date, linebacker Darryl Gamble is the only other Georgia player in the modern era who has returned two interceptions for touchdowns in a single game. It has been done only two other times in SEC history. In fact, only once in NCAA annals has a player returned three interceptions for scores in a game—Houston's Johnny Jackson versus Texas in 1987.

It seems safe to contend that no interception return in Georgia football and few in college football history were as spectacular as Scott's second against Kentucky in 1968. As he turned and churned through the Kentucky offense after making the interception, Scott later admitted he did not think he would score. Nevertheless, nothing could stop the great Scott as he journeyed down the sideline for a 35-yard touchdown.

BILL STANFILL

Bill Stanfill first made a name for himself at Georgia as the only non-junior and non-senior defensive starter on the Bulldogs' 1966 SEC title team. Against Florida that season, Stanfill harassed eventual Heisman Trophy winner Steve Spurrier the entire game, sacking the quarterback several times and forcing turnovers in a 27-10 Georgia victory.

Standout performances in 1968, like in the Kentucky game, led to Stanfill being chosen first-team consensus All-American and Georgia's only Outland Trophy recipient as college football's most outstanding interior lineman.

Against Kentucky in '68, Stanfill, as he did much of his Georgia and eight-year professional football career, played injured. As was the case with other teammates, Stanfill was suffering from boils on his leg. It seems that six weeks before, when Georgia faced Tennessee on its Tartan Turf, small slivers of the synthetic grass were imbedded into the legs of several Bulldogs players, causing the painful inflammation.

TONY TAKES IT TO THE HOUSE

Tony Taylor takes fumbled football away from Georgia Tech in 2006 and scampers 29 yards for a score

Following a 5–0 start to the 2006 season, Georgia lost four of its next five games; the Bulldogs' 6–4 record was their worst after 10 games in 10 years. The chance for a satisfactory season seemed doubtful, as Georgia was to finish the year against Auburn and Georgia Tech.

Surprisingly, the Bulldogs stunned the fifth-ranked Tigers 37–15 on the road and returned home to host the Yellow Jackets. The Bulldogs had defeated their intrastate rival five consecutive times; however, No. 16 Georgia Tech had its best team in years, having already clinched a spot in the Atlantic Coast Conference Championship Game for a bid to play in the Orange Bowl.

In a defensive standoff, the Bulldogs trailed the Yellow Jackets 3–0 late in the third quarter. Georgia Tech lined up in a shotgun formation on its own 27-yard line, facing third down and 15. Quarterback Reggie Ball took the snap, dropped back to his 15-yard line, and then rolled to his right. He decided to keep the football, turned upfield, and ran by Georgia's Marcus Howard. Howard trailed Ball and tackled him from behind, knocking the ball loose close to the 30-yard line. Seconds later, approximately 15 players were fighting for the fumbled ball or peering into the pile. As most of the players nonchalantly stood around, Georgia's Tony Taylor emerged from the massive huddle with the football. The senior linebacker raced to the right of the pile toward the goal line and then dove from the 2-yard line into the end zone, completing a 29-yard fumble return for a touchdown.

Tony Taylor's 29-yard fumble return for a touchdown against Georgia Tech in 2006 is capped with a celebratory dive into the end zone. *Photo courtesy of AP Images.*

Most of the players and coaches on both teams and the sellout crowd in Sanford Stadium had hardly seen what had taken place. The play was reviewed by the replay booth. Surely, the play had been stopped prior to the touchdown return, or Taylor was down before snatching the football out of the pile. Nevertheless, the call on the field, a Georgia touchdown, was confirmed. The Bulldogs added the extra point and led for the first time, 7–3, with 3:10 remaining in the quarter.

MATTHEW STAFFORD

Quarterback Matthew Stafford from Dallas, Texas, was perhaps the second-most highly recruited player in Georgia football history behind only Herschel Walker. An injury to Joe Tereshinski forced Stafford into significant playing time amidst the Bulldogs' four losses in five games during the 2006 season. Stafford struggled until the Auburn game, when he finally came into his own, passing for 219 yards and rushing for 83 against one of college football's best defenses in a 22-point Georgia upset.

Against Georgia Tech, Stafford played opposite Yellow Jackets quarterback Reggie Ball. Ball, a senior looking for his first win over Georgia, suffered mightily, completing just six of 22 passes for 42 yards and turning the ball over on three occasions. Stafford, a true freshman, led the Bulldogs to the game-winning score in the final minutes. In the final game of his freshman campaign, Stafford was named Offensive Most Valuable Player in a 31–24 win over Virginia Tech in the 2006 Chick-fil-A Bowl.

Stafford rode the momentum of the end of his initial year at Georgia into the 2007 season. After a 4–2 start, the sophomore was instrumental in the Bulldogs winning their final seven games, including the 2008 Sugar Bowl, and finishing ranked second in the nation in the Associated Press Poll. His 7,731 career passing yards rank fourth in school history. After leaving school following his junior season, he was the first overall pick in the 2009 NFL draft by the Detroit Lions.

True freshman quarterback Matthew Stafford guided the Bulldogs 64 yards in 12 plays for a touchdown to defeat the Yellow Jackets in the final minutes. *Photo courtesy of AP Images.*

Tony Taylor finished his Bulldogs career with 272 tackles and 10 interceptions. *Photo courtesy of AP Images.*

The Yellow Jackets would build a 12–7 advantage late in the final quarter. Freshman quarterback Matthew Stafford responded by directing the Bulldogs on a 12-play, 64-yard drive that culminated with a four-yard touchdown pass to Mohamed Massaquoi with only 1:45 left to play. A two-point conversion gave Georgia a 15–12 lead. On the ensuing drive, Paul Oliver intercepted Ball to clinch the Bulldogs' eighth win of the year and the sixth consecutive victory over the Yellow Jackets.

Taylor, who grew up just outside of Athens, Georgia, and whose father also played linebacker for Georgia, brought excitement to an otherwise drudging ballgame. His fumble return also added to the long line of controversial plays in the series' nearly 100-game history.

As Ball fumbled forward, it appeared that Georgia Tech right guard Nate McManus had fallen on the ball. The Yellow Jackets said it was clear that McManus' knee was down; however, the officials (an ACC officiating crew) saw differently. As time seemed to stand still, the referees gazed into the pile, looking to see who recovered Ball's fumble, but they never blew a whistle or marked the ball dead. While Tech exclaimed that Taylor pried or yanked the football from a downed McManus, the Georgia linebacker stated the football was lying "two centimeters" from the leg of a Yellow Jacket. Taylor, who later admitted

Game Details

Georgia 15 • Georgia Tech 12

Date: November 25, 2006

Site: Sanford Stadium

Attendance: 92,746

Records: Georgia 7–4; Georgia Tech 9–2

Rankings: Georgia Tech: No. 16 (AP)/No. 15 (USA Today)

Series: Georgia 57–36–5 (Georgia five-game winning streak)

> I got nothing to say on that, dog (in regard to his fumble returned for a touchdown by Taylor).
>
> **—Reggie Ball, Georgia Tech quarterback**

TONY TAYLOR

When Tony Taylor arrived in Athens as a freshman from nearby Watkinsville, Georgia, he had much to live up to. Tony's father, Nate, was an undersized but overachieving linebacker at Georgia from 1979 to 1982. Nate started all four seasons as a Bulldog and still ranks fifth at Georgia in career tackles.

Tony was also a smaller but tenacious linebacker for the Bulldogs, starting as only a sophomore in 2003. After missing the '04 season because of an injury, Taylor returned to start at middle linebacker in 2005 and would then lead the team in tackles the following year as a senior. Taylor's nine tackles and two interceptions earned him the Defensive Most Valuable Player Award of the 2006 Chick-fil-A Bowl.

In 2006, against Ole Miss, Tony Taylor (No. 43) is on the verge of recording one of his 11 tackles against the Rebels in a 14-9 victory. He finished his senior season with a team-high 96 tackles. From his linebacker position, Taylor also intercepted seven passes, leading the nation among nondefensive backs. *Photo courtesy of AP Images.*

His 272 career tackles and 10 interceptions are tied for 21st and 13th, respectively, for all time at Georgia. Taylor's seven interceptions in 2006 were the most in the nation of all nondefensive backs, while his 10 career interceptions are the most ever among nondefensive backs at Georgia. Importantly, Taylor, like his father, played on Bulldogs teams that were a perfect 4–0 against Georgia Tech (like father, like son).

An undrafted free agent by Atlanta of the NFL, Taylor played in all of the Falcons' 16 games in 2007, his only season in the league, recording 12 tackles (11 solo).

he thought for certain the officials would blow his fumble return dead, simply picked up the ball and headed for the end zone.

In 1978 Georgia was given a second chance to defeat Georgia Tech on a contestable pass interference called on a two-point conversion. In 1997 a pass-interference penalty on the Yellow Jackets negated a game-clinching interception and led to Mike Bobo's winning touchdown pass to Corey Allen. In both 1998 and 1999, a controversial fumble and nonfumble were the deciding factors in Georgia Tech victories over Georgia.

One of the greatest plays in Georgia football history, Taylor's touchdown return may be added to the list of questionable calls that helped determine the winner in this bitter rivalry.

POST-HERSCHEL HOUNDS BITE BRUINS

Charlie Dean's touchdown return in final seconds clinches season opener of 1983

Both Georgia and UCLA entered their season-opening meeting in 1983 seemingly less competitve compared to their previous seasons. The Bruins, Pac-10 and Rose Bowl champions in 1982, had lost quarterback Tom Ramsey—an all-conference performer and college football's highest-rated passer the year before. Replacement Rick Neuheisel, a fifth-year senior, had played sparingly in college and was one of 10 UCLA players making their initial start ever as a Bruin. Georgia had lost seven starters on defense, including All-SEC safety Jeff Sanchez, who had broken his arm in preseason practice. The Bulldogs' offensive line, considered the team's strength, was also banged up. Most importantly, gone was tailback Herschel Walker—the predominant reason Georgia achieved a 33–3

Charlie Dean (No. 18) is congratulated by teammates following his game-clinching interception return for a touchdown against UCLA in 1983. *Photo courtesy of Wingate Downs.*

record and three SEC titles from 1980 to 1982 and undoubtedly the school's greatest player in history.

The Walker-less 'Dogs led the Bruins 12–8 with 33 seconds remaining in the game. UCLA was advancing toward Georgia's goal and a possible victory, with a first down on the Bulldogs' 31-yard line.

Rick Neuheisel took the snap from center and first looked to throw deep against the Georgia secondary. Despite the Bulldogs having only 10 men on the field, Neuheisel was forced to pass to his second option. Lined up to Neuheisel's left, tight end Paul Bergman ran a short flare pattern. Immediately prior to Neuheisel's toss reaching Bergman, Charlie Dean appeared from nowhere. The senior safety-man snared the errant pass at his own 26 and raced without interruption down the field into UCLA's end zone.

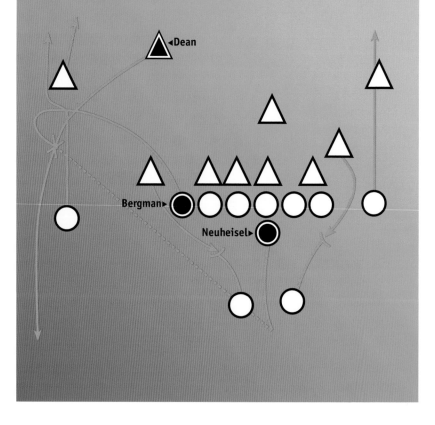

Neuheisel dropped back to throw and floated a pass to his left toward tight end Paul Bergman. Suddenly, Charlie Dean, a native Athenian and playing only because of Sanchez's season-ending injury, stepped in front of the intended receiver. The senior safety intercepted Neuheisel's pass at his 26-yard line and raced untouched down the sideline. Dean's interception return for a touchdown secured a 19–8 victory over UCLA.

In a driving rainstorm, Georgia held a comfortable 12–0 second-quarter lead only to allow two Bruins field goals prior to halftime. The

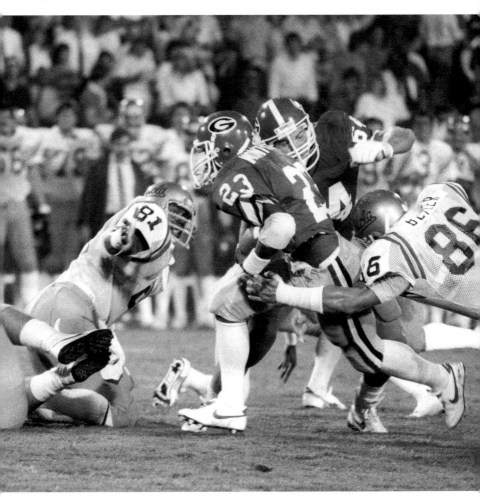

With Herschel Walker no longer in the Bulldogs lineup, Keith Montgomery (No. 23) was one of four tailbacks Georgia tried against the Bruins. *Photo courtesy of Wingate Downs.*

Game Details

Georgia 19 • UCLA 8

Date: September 3, 1983

Site: Sanford Stadium

Attendance: 82,122

Records: Georgia 0-0; UCLA 0-0

Rankings: Georgia: No. 15 (AP)/ No. 13 (UPI); UCLA: No. 20 (AP)/ No. 12 (UPI)

Series: Georgia 1-0 (Georgia one-game winning streak)

> I baited [UCLA's Paul Bergman].... I hung back and waited and hoped they'd [pass] to him again, and they did.
>
> —**Charlie Dean, safety**

Bulldogs' offense was extremely sluggish in the second half, scoring no points. Georgia finished the game with only 59 passing yards, while four tailbacks, Walker's replacements, combined to rush for 102 yards and just 3.6 yards per carry. Scott Williams, a fullback, finished as Georgia's leading rusher.

Twice in the final half UCLA reached inside Georgia's 10-yard line but came away with no points. Included was a Neuheisel pass broken up by cornerback Darryl Jones in the end zone on fourth down and goal from the Bulldogs' 9-yard line with only 2:14 left in the contest.

After Jones' game-saving breakup, Georgia ran three plays and took an intentional safety instead of punting to the Bruins and likely giving them excellent field position. Trailing 12–8, UCLA returned the ensuing kickoff to its own 35-yard line.

With only 1:01 showing on the clock, the Bruins quickly ran four plays, moving the ball to Georgia's 31-yard line. On first and 10, Neuheisel first looked to throw deep, but no Bruin was open against the Dogs' straight man-on-man coverage. Incidentally, Georgia had only 10 defenders on the field. As Bergman flared to his left, Neuheisel looked to throw to the tight end. Baiting the quarterback, Dean laid off Bergman approximately five to six yards. Just as the pass was thrown, Dean closed in on the tight end and intercepted Neuheisel.

"It was really a relief to see Charlie Dean take the ball and run down the field," said Coach Vince Dooley following the game. And run down the field Dean did, lifting his left hand in the air around UCLA's 25-yard line with his index finger pointed upward, proclaiming, "We're number one," as he crossed the Bruins' goal line for a score. The post–Herschel Walker era had officially begun in fine fashion, due in large part to a magnificent interception return by a little-known hometown hero.

CHARLIE DEAN

Charlie Dean was a member of Georgia's junior varsity as a freshman in 1980 and saw limited playing time as a reserve varsity defensive back in 1981 and 1982. He was considered a backup again for his senior year until Jeff Sanchez was lost for the season to an injury. Dean made the most of his starting safety assignment by tying for the team lead in interceptions with three, despite missing two full games with injuries. The most notable of Dean's five career interceptions, the scoring return against UCLA, is perhaps the greatest interception return for a touchdown in Georgia football history.

Along with 13 others, including Georgia football dignitaries Dan Magill and Richard Appleby, Dean was inducted into the Athens Athletic Hall of Fame in 2001. His induction was mostly because Dean quarterbacked Clarke Central High School to a state championship in 1979 and because of his game-clinching touchdown return in 1983 against the Bruins.

MOMENTUM CHANGER IN KNOXVILLE

Sean Jones returns Tennessee fumble 92 yards as first half expires

During the coaching careers of Ray Goff and Jim Donnan at Georgia, the Bulldogs were essentially a second-rate team compared to Tennessee and Florida in the SEC East. Whereas the Volunteers and Gators annually battled for the divisional title, the Bulldogs always seemed to be hoping to land a respectable bowl bid while fighting for third place in the East.

Running back Jabari Davis of Stone Mountain, Georgia, said that he chose to attend school and play football at Tennessee because "Georgia was always talking about getting to the Peach Bowl." According to Davis, Tennessee, on the other hand, had loftier goals like the Rose Bowl.

In 2000 the Bulldogs defeated the Volunteers for the first time since 1988, ending a nine-game winning streak for Tennessee. Head coach Mark Richt arrived in 2001 and upset the Volunteers on the road. The following season, Georgia defeated Tennessee 18–13 en route to the Bulldogs' first SEC title in 20 years. Despite the fact that the

All-American Sean Jones, pictured during the 2003 SEC Championship Game, made several big plays during his three-season tenure at Georgia. None, however, were greater than his 92-yard fumble return against Tennessee in 2003. *Photo courtesy of Getty Images.*

Bulldogs had overtaken Tennessee and Florida as the preeminent team in the division, Georgia apparently still received little respect from some of its opposition.

Tennessee quarterback Casey Clausen missed the 2002 Georgia game with a fractured collarbone. Following his team's loss, Clausen commented that if he had played, the Volunteers would have won by a "couple of touchdowns," and he could have beaten Georgia with one arm tied behind his back. In 2003 both Clausen and Davis would have their final chance together to face the Bulldogs to see if their actions could speak as loud as their words.

Tennessee trailed Georgia 13–7 with only seven seconds remaining until halftime but had the ball inches from the Bulldogs' goal line. On third down and goal, Clausen took the snap and turned to his right to hand the ball to Davis. Fullback Troy Fleming, in attempting to run through the line to block, accidentally bumped Clausen's hand, and the ball was fumbled around the 5-yard line. Clausen and Georgia free safety Thomas Davis dove for the football but crashed into one another. The bobbled ball rolled right into the path of roverback Sean Jones. Jones scooped up the fumble at the 8-yard line and started down his left sideline. With a convoy of blockers, Jones streaked 92 yards into the end zone as time expired in the first half.

Game Details

Georgia 41 • Tennessee 14

Date: October 11, 2003

Site: Neyland Stadium

Attendance: 107,517

Records: Georgia 4–1; Tennessee 4–1

Rankings: Georgia: No. 8 (AP)/ No. 10 (ESPN); Tennessee: No. 13 (AP)/ No. 14 (ESPN)

Series: Tennessee 17-13-2 (Georgia three-game winning streak)

> [Jones' return] was probably the biggest momentum changer I've ever seen in a big game.
>
> **—Mark Richt, Georgia head coach**

In an attempt to block for his teammate, Tennessee fullback Troy Fleming inadvertently bumped quarterback Casey Clausen's hand before the quarterback's handoff was received by Jabari Davis. The ball was fumbled and trickled toward the right of the offense. At the 6 Georgia's Thomas Davis attempted to pick up the fumble, but a diving Clausen knocked the ball loose. However, the fumble rolled directly in front of roverback Sean Jones, who picked up the football at the 8. Aided by a host of Bulldogs blockers as time ran out in the first half, Jones sprinted for pay dirt with no Volunteers remotely near him.

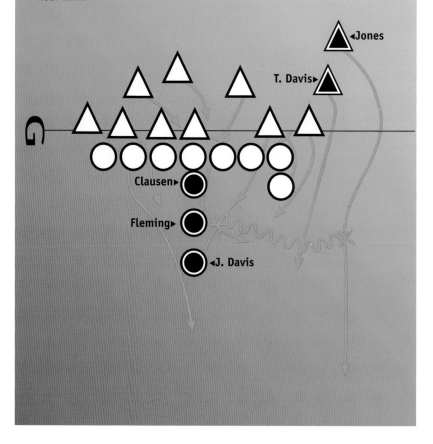

An injured Casey Clausen looks on in disgust as Tennessee is beaten by Georgia in 2002. The Volunteers never defeated the Bulldogs with Clausen at quarterback, including a devastating 41–14 loss in 2003. *Photo courtesy of AP Images.*

What should have been a one-point advantage for Tennessee at halftime was instead a 20–7 comfortable lead for Georgia. The Bulldogs kept their momentum through the half and into the third quarter, scoring three rushing touchdowns in a span of only 2:35 and eventually winning, 41–14. For the first time in history, Georgia defeated the Volunteers four consecutive seasons.

The Bulldogs had a 10–0 second-quarter lead until Clausen connected with Mark Jones for a 90-yard touchdown—a Tennessee record for longest pass play. Georgia's Billy Bennett kicked a field goal with 3:27 left in the quarter and gave the Bulldogs a six-point lead. In the final minutes, the Volunteers moved 87 yards in 11 plays. During the drive, Georgia committed two personal foul penalties by defenders

BRIAN VANGORDER

Brian VanGorder arrived at Georgia in 2001, along with a newly hired Mark Richt. After Georgia's defenses had been above average at best for most of the previous several years, VanGorder's defensive unit instantly began making its presence known. After ranking fourth in the country in scoring defense in 2002, the Bulldogs finished in the nation's top 10 in both total and scoring defense in 2003 and 2004. VanGorder coached six Bulldogs defenders, including Sean Jones, selected in the first two rounds of the NFL draft. In 2003 VanGorder was honored as the nation's top assistant coach.

Following the 2004 season VanGorder left Georgia and made a seemingly lateral move to coach linebackers for the Jacksonville Jaguars. Since 2005 VanGorder has held seven different positions in both the NFL and college football and is currently Notre Dame's defensive coordinator.

The fiery, well-respected, and well-liked VanGorder was unfortunately a Bulldog for only four seasons. Nevertheless, he may be the best of the 10 defensive coordinators Georgia has had since Erk Russell departed in 1980.

SEAN JONES

During the University of Tennessee's last drive before halftime of the 2003 game, Sean Jones committed one of Georgia's two costly personal fouls. The penalty by Jones infuriated defensive coordinator Brian VanGorder to the point where the coach stepped from the sideline and literally slapped Jones upside his helmet. VanGorder must have slapped some sense into Jones as, moments later, the roverback was aware enough to recover a Tennessee fumble and race 92 yards for a score.

Jones culminated three seasons at Georgia by being selected consensus All-SEC and first-team All-American in 2003 by the American Football Coaches Association. In his collegiate career, Jones recorded 250 tackles, 10 tackles for loss, 10 passes broken up, seven interceptions, and four blocked kicks. His 16.0 career punt return average (160 yards on 10 returns—all in 2002) ranks second in school history among players with at least 10 career returns.

Jones came out of college early following his junior campaign to enter the NFL draft. A second-round selection by Cleveland, he sat out the 2004 season with a knee injury. By his third season, he was starting at strong safety for the Browns. His seven-year NFL career also included stints with Philadelphia and Tampa Bay.

Odell Thurman and Sean Jones within four plays of one another. The latter penalty moved Tennessee to the Bulldogs' 14-yard line with approximately 1:30 left on the clock. Three plays later, Cedric Houston rushed for two yards on first down to Georgia's 1-yard line. On second down, coach Phillip Fulmer called for Clausen to spike the ball to stop the clock. Instead, the quarterback sneaked for no gain. Because of the miscommunication, Tennessee was forced to call its final timeout of the first half with seven seconds remaining.

Only inches from tying the contest, the Volunteers lined up in their "jumbo package"—three tight ends and their two big backs: Davis (225 pounds) and Fleming (230). In hindsight, Tennessee should have selected a different package, as its special formation lost a game-changing fumble and yielded Sean Jones' magnificent 92-yard return.

During their careers at Tennessee, Clausen and Davis never defeated Georgia when seeing significant playing time in meetings between the rivals. Clausen, who always played with both arms against the Bulldogs, relieved A.J. Suggs in 2000 in a losing effort, and he started against Georgia and lost in 2001 and 2003. Davis saw action against the 'Dogs in 2002 and 2003. In those same seasons, he participated in the only two bowl games he experienced as a Volunteer—both losses in the Peach Bowl.

TERRY TIPS AWAY TOUCHDOWN

Terry Hoage tips a sure Vanderbilt touchdown in 1983 to help secure victory

Entering the 44th meeting between Georgia and Vanderbilt, the Bulldogs had defeated the Commodores nine straight times and had lost just once since 1961. However, the '83 Vandy squad was not necessarily the Commodores of old. It had won eight games the year before, and although Vanderbilt had a 2–3 record, all three of the losses were to nationally ranked opponents. The Commodores exhibited a high-powered passing attack, averaging more than 300 yards per game, ranking fourth in the nation. Undefeated Georgia hoped to become Vandy's fourth loss to a ranked opponent, but a victory would not be easy for the Bulldogs.

Georgia's Terry Hoage emerged in 1982 as one of the most outstanding defensive players in school history. He led the nation in interceptions with 12, including a school-record three against Vanderbilt. By 1983 the senior roverback was touted as arguably college football's greatest defensive back. A week prior to the Vandy game,

After his pass deflection broke up a potential game-winning touchdown pass against Vanderbilt in 1983, Terry Hoage (No. 14) celebrates with cornerback Darryl Jones (No. 17). *Photo courtesy of Wingate Downs.*

> Where did he come from? I thought it was a touchdown all the way.
>
> **—Kurt Page, Vanderbilt quarterback**

Hoage missed the Ole Miss contest with an injury and practiced only one day the following week. Against the Commodores, the consensus All-American would play out of position at safety, filling in for an injured Charlie Dean. Hoage and the rest of Georgia's pass defenders had their hands full against the Commodores' feared passing game.

Trailing the Bulldogs by only seven points with approximately 30 seconds left in the game, Vanderbilt was within striking distance to possibly hand Georgia its first loss of the season. Deep in Georgia territory, quarterback Kurt Page was chased out of the pocket and rolled to his right. He lofted a pass to split end Joe Kelly, who was wide open in the far right corner of the end zone. Just as Kelly opened his arms to make the catch, Hoage appeared out of nowhere, and leaping as high as he could, tipped the ball. Falling backward in the end zone in front of Kelly, Hoage had succeeded in breaking up a touchdown.

Earlier in the first half, Georgia's Keith Montgomery scored two touchdowns; however, two turnovers by backup quarterback Todd Williams led to 10 Vanderbilt points, and the Commodores trailed by only four at halftime.

Vanderbilt kicked a third-quarter field goal and pulled within a point. Kevin Butler countered with two field goals, the second giving Georgia a 20–13 lead with 1:41 remaining in the contest.

Despite the Bulldogs often placing eight defenders in pass coverage, they could not stop Page's passing prowess. In the game, the junior quarterback threw for more than 300 yards on 33 of 56 passes. Commodore Keith Edwards finished with 17 receptions—a Southeastern Conference record that stood for 18 years. Prior to Vandy's final drive, Page had thrown three interceptions, including one corralled by Hoage in the second quarter on the Bulldogs' 16-yard line.

In the final two minutes of play and trailing by a touchdown, Page drove the Commodores to Georgia's 24-yard line. On second down and 10 to go, Page threw what appeared to be the perfect pass. Kelly, running a post route to the corner of the end zone, was also in the apparent perfect place. Attempting to cover the intended receiver, Hoage first slipped and fell on the artificial turf. Picking himself up, he ran toward Kelly and arrived at the very last moment to tip away Page's pass. Two plays later, Andre Holmes intercepted Page on the goal line, conserving the Bulldogs' seven-point lead.

Following Georgia's 20–13 victory, coach Vince Dooley said the leaping pass breakup was the greatest play he had ever seen and that Hoage was the best defensive player he had coached in his 20 years at Georgia.

Game Details

Georgia 20 • Vanderbilt 13

Date: October 15, 1983

Site: Vanderbilt Stadium

Attendance: 41,223

Records: Georgia 4-0-1; Vanderbilt 2-3

Rankings: Georgia: No. 8 (AP)/ No. 6 (UPI)

Series: Georgia 27-15-1 (Georgia nine-game winning streak)

> I don't know if I'd made it if the quarterback hadn't floated the ball just a little bit.
>
> **—Terry Hoage, defensive back**

TERRY HOAGE

Terry Hoage played most of his senior year in 1983 with tendinitis or injuries to his ankle or knee. He was forced to miss three entire games and only started five for the season. When he was able to participate, Hoage often played out of position because of other injuries to Georgia's secondary. After intercepting 12 passes as a junior, Hoage was limited to two in 1983.

By the end of the 1982 season, Terry Hoage, who intercepted 12 passes during the year, was considered one of the greatest defenders in college football. In his senior campaign of 1983, Hoage finished fifth in the Heisman Trophy voting, despite missing three games and only starting in five during the season. *Photo courtesy of AP Images.*

Despite these circumstances, Hoage was selected consensus All-American for a second time and remarkably finished fifth in the Heisman Trophy voting. These accolades are a tribute to how valuable Hoage was to the Bulldogs despite his injuries. Whether it was making 16 tackles and two sacks in the season opener against UCLA, blocking two field goals against Clemson to help preserve a tie, or breaking up Vanderbilt's potential game-tying touchdown, Hoage seemed to always make pivotal plays for Georgia in 1983.

After playing 12 years in the NFL, recording 21 interceptions and two touchdowns (one rushing!), Hoage was elected into the College Football Hall of Fame in 2000 and the CoSIDA Academic All-American Hall of Fame in 2004. He currently owns and operates Terry Hoage Vineyards in Paso Robles, California.

Terry Hoage (center) is mobbed by several Georgia defenders, celebrating his breakup of the Commodores' pass into the end zone. *Photo courtesy of Wingate Downs.*

POLLACK'S MIDAIR SCORING STRIP

David Pollack amazingly seizes football from Gamecocks quarterback throwing from out of his own end zone

Led by quarterback David Greene, running back Musa Smith, five senior offensive linemen, and several excellent receivers, Georgia's offense in 2002 was one of the best in recent memory. However, when the Bulldogs encountered South Carolina on the road in Columbia, the Gamecocks' pesky defense and the effects of Tropical Storm Hanna slowed the Georgia offense to a crawl. The Bulldogs ended their game still not having scored an offensive touchdown against South Carolina since the first quarter two meetings prior in 2000. Nonetheless, Georgia was victorious, requiring something other than its offense: a defensive play that defies comprehension.

In a defensive standoff, Georgia led South Carolina 3–0 early in the final quarter. Facing second down from his own 7-yard line, South Carolina quarterback Corey Jenkins rolled to his

David Pollack celebrates after scoring his miraculous touchdown against South Carolina in 2002 where he stripped the opposing quarterback of the football in the end zone. *Photo courtesy of AP Images.*

DAVID POLLACK

David Pollack arrived at Georgia as a little-known fullback prospect in 2001. By the second game of his sophomore season of 2002 against South Carolina, he had quickly established himself as one of the best and most relentless defensive linemen in college football. Against the Gamecocks, Pollack recorded 14 tackles, recovered a fumble, and made one of the most incredible touchdowns in recent memory in all of football. He was named CBS Player of the Game and Southeastern Conference Defensive Player of the Week for his performance. Those honors would be just two of many. Pollack would eventually become the most decorated player, besides Herschel Walker, in Georgia football history.

Pollack rests on the sideline following his remarkable touchdown. As only a sophomore, he would eventually be selected the SEC's Most Valuable Player in 2002—the first Bulldog to earn the honor since Garrison Hearst in 1992 and the first defender in 14 years (after Tracy Rocker of Auburn in 1988). *Photo courtesy of Getty Images.*

Pollack was a three-time first-team All-American (2002–2004), was a two-time SEC Defensive Player of the Year (2002, 2004), twice won the Ted Hendricks Award as the nation's top defensive end (2003–2004), received the Rotary Lombardi Award as the nation's top lineman, and received the Chuck Bednarik Award as the nation's top defensive player in 2004.

Pollack's 36 school-record sack total is seven more than the second most in Georgia history (Richard Tardits, 29). He also ranks first at Georgia in career total tackles for loss and quarterback hurries.

Perhaps more than pure athletic ability, Pollack demonstrated an intense and unfaltering demeanor that enabled him to succeed on the gridiron at Georgia for four seasons. He was known to "give it his all" on every single play, his "motor" constantly running in games, and even during practices.

Pollack was the 17th overall selection in the 2005 NFL draft, chosen by the Cincinnati Bengals. In his rookie season he played in 14 games and started five, making 35 tackles and four and a half sacks. During his second game of the following season, Pollack unfortunately suffered a neck fracture that ended his season and his professional football career. Pollack is currently a college football analyst for ESPN.

> I'm just trying to make a play, to get back there [to the quarterback] as fast as I could.
>
> **—David Pollack, Georgia defensive end,**
> **prior to scoring the touchdown**

right, looking downfield to pass. Standing in his own end zone, Jenkins began his throwing motion; Georgia defensive end David Pollack raced toward the Gamecocks quarterback. Pollack jumped in the air as Jenkins threw the football, somehow grabbed and cradled the ball as it was released, and fell to the ground in the end zone still clutching the football—a mind-boggling touchdown that one needs to observe several times before believing it actually occurred.

Pollack, who earlier had recovered a Gamecocks fumble on Georgia's 2-yard line, had energized the team all by himself and had given the Bulldogs a two-score advantage.

A South Carolina touchdown was answered by a Billy Bennett field goal with 2:54 left in the game, and Georgia held a 13–7 lead. The Gamecocks promptly began marching for the game-winning touchdown, moving 71 yards in nine plays to the Bulldogs' 2-yard line.

Game Details

Georgia 13 • South Carolina 7

Date: September 14, 2002

Site: Williams-Brice Stadium

Attendance: 84,227

Records: Georgia 1–0; South Carolina 1–1

Rankings: Georgia: No. 9 (AP)/ No. 10 (ESPN)

Series: Georgia 39–13–2 (South Carolina two-game winning streak)

> Pollack's is the cake-taker for unusual touchdowns.
>
> **—Dan Magill, Georgia football historian**

On fourth down and one with 20 seconds left in the contest, Jenkins' pitch hit running back Andrew Pinnock in the chest. Pinnock's fumble and South Carolina's fourth turnover of the game was recovered by Georgia's Thomas Davis. The Bulldogs ran the remaining 12 seconds off the clock and escaped Williams-Brice Stadium with a win.

Prior to the fourth quarter, the lone highlights of a drudging game were a Bennett field goal early in the opening quarter and a 52-minute delay brought on by the tropical storm—the only time in Georgia football's modern history that a game has been interrupted by the weather.

On the touchdown play, Pollack got around Gamecocks tackle Watts Sanderson and was only trying to get a hand on the ball as he lunged toward the quarterback. He leaped just as Jenkins threw and somehow, some way, was soon clutching the football in South Carolina's end zone. Everyone witnessing this chain of events was beyond bewildered.

Jenkins later commented that after attempting to pass, he assumed that Pollack only knocked the ball to the ground incomplete. Only when he heard someone shout "touchdown" did he realize what had occurred.

Writer Tim Tucker reported that Coach Richt, at that instant, "quietly and wrongly assumed that the refs must have blown the call"; the stripped ball surely hit the ground before Pollack could seize it. The coach would later realize that his star defensive end, in fact, had executed something that Richt would call the greatest defensive play he had ever seen.

SPECIAL
CONSIDERATION

GURLEY'S RETURN ULTIMATELY TAMES TIGERS

Todd Gurley's 100-yard touchdown comes early but proves to be the game's deciding play

In 2013, tailback Todd Gurley put on quite a show at Clemson, rushing for 154 yards and two touchdowns, but it wasn't quite enough to lead Georgia to a victory. Due in large part to the Bulldogs' sub-par play on defense and special teams, Georgia narrowly lost its season-opening game in Death Valley, 38–35. One year later, the Bulldogs-Tigers game in Athens was unfortunately beginning to shape up much like the teams' previous meeting.

After scoring a touchdown midway through the second quarter to take a 21–14 lead, Clemson kicked off to Georgia, seemingly having taken control of the game.

Returning his first kickoff since the third game of the 2012 season, or nearly two entire years before, Gurley received Bradley Pinion's kick halfway into his own end zone and began running straight upfield. After nudging teammate Taylor Maxey in the back to make a block around his own 30-yard line, Gurley slightly cut to his left, and then sped past everyone while nearly going untouched for a 100-yard touchdown return.

What might have seemed at the time as simply a game-tying touchdown with two-and-a-half quarters of play remaining would

Todd Gurley's 100-yard kickoff return galvanized the Bulldogs in the first half of their game against Clemson in 2014. *Photo courtesy of AP Images.*

prove to be arguably the most impactful play executed by a Bulldog in several years, and the catalyst for perhaps the biggest swing in momentum witnessed in Sanford Stadium in decades.

Georgia, which entered its 2014 season opener winners of just seven of 22 games against AP-ranked, top-20 opponents since the start of the 2009 season, had a recent reputation of faltering against stiff competition, and this was apparent early on against 16th-ranked Clemson. After Georgia built a 14–7 advantage, including a scoring run by Gurley, its defense allowed the Tigers consecutive touchdowns—the second resulting from a 10-play drive, in which six plays were run inside the Bulldogs' 7-yard line. Clemson's go-ahead touchdown with 7:28 until halftime seemed to suck the air right out of what had been a raucous, sellout Sanford Stadium crowd.

Game Details

Georgia 45 • Clemson 21

Date: August 30, 2014

Site: Sanford Stadium

Attendance: 92,746

Records: Georgia 0-0; Clemson 0-0

Rankings: Georgia 12th AP/8th Coaches; Clemson 16th AP/24th Coaches

Series: Georgia 41-18-4 (Clemson one-game winning streak)

> It was a game of momentum, and I think by far the biggest play was the kickoff return for a touchdown. It just got us back in it.
>
> **—Mark Richt, Georgia head coach**

TODD GURLEY

With the Clemson game, Todd Gurley began his junior campaign of 2014 like no other Georgia back in decades. Through the season's first five games, he rushed for 773 yards, averaged 8.2 yards per rush, scored nine touchdowns, and even completed a pass for 50 yards. However, just two days before Georgia's sixth game of the year, the Bulldog Nation was dealt a major blow when it was announced the Heisman Trophy front-runner would serve what would be a four-game suspension for violation of NCAA rules.

Gurley had a triumphant return in mid-November, rushing for 138 yards and a touchdown in a 34-7 rout of ninth-ranked Auburn; however, he sustained an ACL injury in the fourth quarter and was out for the season. A little over a month later, Gurley announced he was leaving early for the NFL, thus ending his shortened Georgia career.

For his three-season career, Gurley rushed for 3,285 yards, scored 44 touchdowns—36 via rushing, averaged 109.5 rushing yards per game, while totaling 4,322 all-purpose yards—all of which rank second in Georgia history behind Herschel Walker. Although Todd Gurley's Georgia career is one of preeminence—perhaps the greatest by a Bulldog running back second only to the legendary Walker—missing 10 entire games in 2013 and 2014 combined leaves one wondering what might have been.

Nevertheless, it took only one play to bring the crowd to its feet again, and it lasted for the duration of the game.

Gurley had been positioned as the team's deep man on two previous kickoffs that night, but he appeared apprehensive to return either kicks, each resulting in a touchback. "Coach Ball and Coach Lilly [Georgia's assistants in charge of kickoffs] had a great game plan," Gurley said following the game, "and we knew that we would [eventually] have the middle of the field open."

NICK CHUBB

Standing on the sideline at the time, Nick Chubb had absolutely nothing to do with Todd Gurley's dynamic kickoff return against Clemson. However, it was against the Tigers that Chubb made his debut as a Bulldog, and it would be in relief of Gurley the freshman tailback had one of the finest first-year campaigns in Georgia football history.

Beginning with the Clemson game, when he rushed for 70 yards on only four carries, including a tackle-breaking 47-yard jaunt for a touchdown, Chubb averaged approximately 45 yards on only six rushes per contest as Gurley's backup. However, as soon as Gurley began serving a suspension for NCAA rules violations, it was "Chubby Time" as the freshman phenom began a rushing spree exceeded at Georgia only by Herschel Walker.

In the final eight games of the 2014 season, Chubb averaged 165.4 rushing yards per contest, 7.0 yards per carry, and scored 12 touchdowns. He had two 200-yard rushing performances, including 266 yards in a 37–14 victory over Louisville in the Belk Bowl—the second-most rushing yards in a game by an individual in Bulldog history.

Notwithstanding, for Georgia fans entering the 2015 season, the most important figure concerning their new prized tailback is *at least two*—or, the number of seasons Chubb has remaining as a member of the Bulldogs.

Finally, the middle of the field was open for Gurley on a kickoff, and it didn't matter he was standing about five yards deep in his own end zone upon receiving the kick. "We made a commitment this week that even if it was three, four, five, even six yards deep, we were coming out of there," said Georgia head coach Mark Richt.

Gurley indeed came out of there. Patiently allowing a wall of blockers to form in front of him, the junior speedster located an opening up the middle, and promptly outraced all pursuing Tigers into the end zone. For Gurley, who had also returned a kickoff 100 yards for a touchdown in the 2012 season opener against Buffalo, it was his second 100-yard kickoff return in just eight career returns as a Bulldog.

After tying the score at 21–21, Georgia carried the momentum through halftime and into the second half. As much as the first half was a back-and-forth slugfest, the rest of the game was very much a one-sided affair. After allowing 14 first downs and 276 total yards in the first half to Clemson, the Bulldog defense remarkably yielded just one first down and 15 yards following intermission.

With Georgia leading 24–21 early in the fourth quarter, Gurley scored his third touchdown on an 18-yard run. Less than two minutes later, true freshman Nick Chubb had a spectacular 47-yard touchdown run in which he broke multiple tackles en route to the end zone. With 7:34 remaining in the contest, Gurley put the icing on the cake of a 45–21 victory by scoring his fourth and final touchdown on a 51-yard sprint.

"That's probably one of our biggest wins," said Gurley, who gained a school-record 293 all-purpose yards, including a then-career-high 198 rushing yards on 15 carries. "[Our defense] just stopped them from scoring [in the second half]; if they don't score, they can't win." And likewise, if Gurley doesn't run back the second-quarter kickoff for a score, perhaps Clemson wins.

> I just had to get [to the middle of the field on my kickoff return] and get through the hole. Luckily I was able to do that and I just kept running.
>
> **—Todd Gurley, Georgia tailback**

A ONE-MAN SHOW

Highlighted by a recovery of his own blocked punt, Charley Trippi nearly single-handedly defeats 'Bama in '46

Prior to the arrival of Herschel Walker, the greatest football player ever at the University of Georgia was arguably Charley Trippi. Trippi made several remarkable runs, passes, returns, and plays on defense during his three years on Georgia's varsity (1942, 1945–1946). Nevertheless, the greatest play he ever pulled off, according to some, including author John Stegeman, is rather unconventional to say the least.

In the second quarter of the 1946 Georgia-Alabama game, the Bulldogs led 7–0; however, Georgia was backed up toward its own goal line, and Trippi was set to punt on third down. His quick kick was blocked by Alabama tackle Charley Compton, and the ball bounded toward the Bulldogs' end zone. Both Charleys ran toward the goal line in mad pursuit and, once inside the 10-yard line, dove simultaneously for the ball. Georgia's Charley made an extraordinary recovery of his own blocked quick kick at the Bulldogs' 6-yard line. Because Georgia had elected to punt on third and not fourth down, it

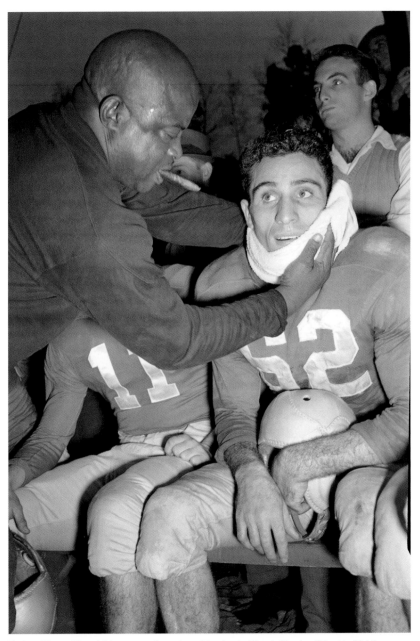

Trainer Harry "Squab" Jones applies a towel to star halfback Charley Trippi in 1946. Trippi's recovery of his own blocked punt that season against Alabama has been called his greatest play. *Photo courtesy of AP Images.*

Just as significant as Charley Trippi's performance against the Crimson Tide in 1946, Alabama's Harry "the Arm" Gilmer's performance, or a lack thereof, was also significant. As a sophomore in '45, Gilmer was named SEC player of the year, finished fifth in the Heisman Trophy voting, and led the Crimson Tide to a perfect 10-0 record, including a 28-14 victory over Georgia in late October. Against the Bulldogs, Gilmer completed 14 of 20 passes for 146 yards and three

Alabama's Harry Gilmer was considered one of the best passers in college football during the 1940s. However, against Georgia in 1946, he did not complete a single pass in eight attempts during a 14-0 loss. *Photo courtesy of Getty Images.*

touchdowns. A year later in '46, the Arm was grounded at Georgia. Although Gilmer led Alabama with 55 rushing yards on 12 carries, he did not complete a single pass in eight attempts and was intercepted twice. Gilmer was recognized as probably the best passer in college football. In more than two and a half seasons at Alabama, he never had a game in which he had not successfully completed at least one pass. The 6', 160-pound quarterback completed 69 passes for the 1946 season—fourth best in the nation.

Gilmer rebounded against the Bulldogs as a senior in 1947. In a 17-7 victory, he completed five of 10 passes and scored the game's first points on an 80-yard punt return. The 52 touchdowns he accounted for while at Alabama remained a school record until 2013. Gilmer played eight seasons in the NFL, was a head coach for two years with Detroit in the mid-1960s, and was inducted into the College Football Hall of Fame in 1993.

retained possession. On the next play, Trippi lofted a lengthy punt out of his own end zone and bailed the Bulldogs out of anticipated danger. It was the third consecutive punt by Trippi from behind his own goal line; he averaged 51 yards per kick.

For only the second time in 32 meetings since 1895, Georgia and Alabama faced off in Athens. The 52,000 in attendance at Sanford Stadium were the most to witness a sporting event in the state of Georgia. On a rain-drenched field, Georgia's Dick McPhee intercepted star Harry Gilmer on the quarterback's first pass of the game. Three plays later, the Bulldogs faced third down and 6 on the Crimson Tide's 9-yard line. Trippi passed into the end zone, and end Dan Edwards made a diving catch of a tipped ball for a touchdown.

> Trippi's scramble with Compton for that blocked kick was really great. Charley's recovery sure pulled us out of a hole.
>
> **—Wally Butts, Georgia head coach**

In the following quarter, Trippi, besides his punt return against Tulsa in the 1946 Oil Bowl, might have executed his greatest play as a collegian. If he had not recovered his own blocked kick, Alabama, regarded as one of the best teams in the nation, likely would have scored a touchdown soon afterward. Instead, the Crimson Tide began their next drive near midfield, where they could not generate any offense.

Prior to halftime, Trippi ran a toss sweep to his right for 46 yards, "tight roping down the sideline to the end zone." As he had accomplished several times before during his two and a half seasons at Georgia, Trippi had given the Bulldogs a comfortable lead nearly by himself. He was attributed the ultimate respect when Alabama's Million Dollar Band spelled out "T-R-I-P-P-I" in his honor at halftime.

Trippi's towering kicks held off the Crimson Tide during the final two quarters. Two of his second-half punts were downed inside Alabama's 10-yard line. Trippi's 38-yard punting average for the game was achieved in booting a soaked football.

Game Details

Georgia 14 • Alabama 0

Date: November 2, 1946

Site: Sanford Stadium

Attendance: 52,000

Records: Georgia 5–0; Alabama 5–1

Rankings: Georgia: No. 5 (AP); Alabama: No. 15 (AP)

Series: Alabama 15-13-3 (Alabama one-game winning streak)

> Trippi was certainly the difference [in Georgia's victory].
>
> **—Vaughn Mancha, Alabama's All-American center**

CHARLEY TRIPPI

Charley Trippi's successful football career continued after his playing days at Georgia. Trippi played for nine seasons in the NFL from 1947 to 1955, all with the Chicago Cardinals. For at least one season, Trippi led Chicago in rushing, passing, receiving, punting, kick returns, and/or punt returns. In 99 career games, he passed for 2,547 yards, rushed for 3,506 and a 5.1 average, caught 130 passes, intercepted four, averaged 13.7 yards per punt return, and averaged 22.1 per kick return. Trippi was responsible for 53 touchdowns during a professional career similar to his stint at Georgia—a "do-it-all" type player. He is only one of four Georgia players to be the first overall selection in the NFL draft (Frank Sinkwich, Harry Babcock, and Matthew Stafford are the others) and just one of two inducted into the Pro Football Hall of Fame (Fran Tarkenton).

After retiring from playing, Trippi was an assistant coach in Chicago for two seasons. He then returned to Georgia and held the same position with the Bulldogs from 1958 to 1962. Trippi finished his coaching career with a second stretch with the Cardinals for three seasons through 1965. He left coaching and became a highly successful businessman in the city where he first flourished. The 93-year-old living legend still resides in Athens, Georgia.

Alabama finished with only 163 total yards (zero passing on nine attempts) in its 14–0 shutout loss to the Bulldogs. Georgia rushed for 139 yards, 98 by Trippi on 16 carries. The Bulldogs' superstar halfback also completed five of 11 passes, throwing for 109 of the game's 110 passing yards. Performing a one-man show, Trippi was responsible for 207 of Georgia's 249 yards, while his punts kept the Crimson Tide from nearing the Bulldogs' goal line, including one that was blocked.

PUNT PINS DOWN GREENIES

Bill Hartman's 44-yard boot against Tulane in 1937 leads to Vassa Cate's scoring return and a victory

The 1937 season began auspiciously for the Georgia Bulldogs as they started 4–1 with only a one-point loss keeping them from perfection at Holy Cross, which would finish the season undefeated and ranked 14th in the nation. However, injuries began to take their toll on the Bulldogs squad, and Georgia suffered shutout losses in its next two ballgames.

The Georgia-Tulane game had been advertised as a battle between the teams' fullbacks: captain Bill Hartman of Georgia and Tulane's "Honest" John Andrews. This was no longer the case, as the veteran Hartman was forced to play quarterback for the first time as a Bulldog because of the rash of injuries.

It was a 44-yard punt by Hartman, however, in the opening quarter that led to Georgia's lone touchdown and a Bulldogs victory. Hartman had several marvelous punts on that day versus Tulane, but none was better than the one pinning

Soon after Hartman's great punt, Vassa Cate (No. 25) returned a Tulane kick 37 yards for a touchdown. *Photo courtesy of Hargrett Rare Book & Manuscript Library/University of Georgia Libraries.*

Tulane near its own goal line—the greatest punt in the history of Georgia football.

Late in the first quarter, Georgia faced fourth down and 1 on the Green Wave's 46-yard line. The Bulldogs were having considerable difficulty moving the football, so coach Harry Mehre elected to punt the ball instead of going for the first down. Precision punting by Hartman resulted in the 44-yard kick going out of bounds at Tulane's 2-yard line.

More than 75 years ago, before most football offenses began utilizing a passing attack and sustaining long offensive drives via the run and pass, teams would often punt prior to fourth down if backed up close to their goal line. On first down on its own 2-yard line, Tulane's Stanley Nyhan punted to Vassa Cate. Cate, a 165-pound sophomore, took the punt on the Green Wave 37-yard line, twisted and wove his way through would-be tacklers, and headed down the left sideline abetted by excellent blocking for a touchdown. Billy Mims' point-after try was successful, and the Bulldogs had an early 7–0 lead. Cate's return was one of only two Bulldogs touchdowns in five games from October 30 until December 10.

Tulane missed out on several scoring opportunities during the contest. Just before halftime, Tulane's Bill "Dub" Mathis was dropped

BILL HARTMAN

Considered one of college football's most underrated players at the time, the versatile Bill Hartman played quarterback against Tulane because of injuries and won the game with his punting.

Two weeks later against Georgia Tech, it was Hartman again who was responsible for the Bulldogs' points. He returned the second-half kickoff 93 yards for a touchdown in a 6–6 tie with the favored Yellow Jackets. Georgia Tech certainly would have scored more if not for Hartman's punting. Kicking a rain-soaked, heavy football, he averaged 42 yards on 15 punts.

Hartman played one season in the NFL and returned to Georgia in 1939 as an assistant and volunteer kicking coach for 36 seasons through 1994. Hartman is well remembered as one of the most beloved Bulldogs ever and as a man who put the University of Georgia and its football program ahead of his personal interests.

Prior to becoming an assistant coach at Georgia for 36 seasons through 1994, Bill Hartman was a standout fullback for the Bulldogs. An All-American in 1937, Hartman's extraordinary punting against Tulane led to a 7–6 Georgia win. *Photo courtesy of AP Images.*

for a three-yard loss by Marvin Gillespie on fourth and goal from inside Georgia's 1-yard line. In the third quarter, Tulane again reached inside the Bulldogs' 4-yard line but came up empty.

With 12 minutes remaining in the game, Tulane finally scored on a touchdown pass; however, Mathis' point after was blocked by John Davis, preserving Georgia's one-point lead. The Green Wave's two final possessions ended with interceptions: Jim Cavan picked off a pass in his own end zone, and Walter Troutman clinched the upset win with an interception at his own 20-yard line.

The Bulldogs offense struggled, gaining only four total yards and one first down during the entire game. In comparison, Tulane, in a losing effort, had 228 yards and 12 first downs.

Without a doubt, it was Hartman's punting that won the game for the Bulldogs. He averaged 40 yards per kick on 17 punts, including a long punt of 72. Most importantly, it was Hartman's first-quarter, 44-yard punt that went out of bounds at the 2-yard line that led to an eventual 7–6 Georgia victory.

Game Details

Georgia 7 • Tulane 6

Date: November 13, 1937

Site: Sanford Stadium

Attendance: 13,000

Records: Georgia 4-3; Tulane 4-2-1

Series: Tied 5-5-1 (Georgia two-game winning streak)

> It is the best game I have ever seen a Georgia team play against a superior team.
>
> **—Harry Mehre, Georgia head coach**

HARRY MEHRE

The 1937 season was the final of 10 years spent by Harry Mehre as Georgia's head coach before he left to coach Ole Miss from 1938 to 1942 and 1944 to 1945. Although the '37 campaign was not one of his most successful years at Georgia, it was arguably Mehre's best coaching effort.

The Bulldogs entered the last month of the season marred with injuries and facing superior opposition. Mehre's squad responded without a loss, defeating Tulane and Miami of Florida and tying Auburn and Georgia Tech to finish 6-3-2 for the season.

Mehre still ranks fourth at Georgia in all-time coaching victories with 59. Importantly, he was known as a coach who always had his Bulldogs well prepared for the big games. During his tenure, Georgia achieved a 6-2-2 record against Georgia Tech and was 8-3-1 against the eastern elite: Fordham, New York University, and Yale.

THE RETURNER'S LONG JAUNT

Scott "the Returner" Woerner intercepts Clemson's Homer Jordan and runs 98 yards down the sideline

Professional scouts came to Athens for the Georgia-Clemson game in 1980 primarily to observe Bulldogs senior Scott Woerner. The All-American candidate at cornerback was selected defensive captain for the game; however, there was a slight issue. Woerner was not starting and had been demoted to back up Greg Bell. By his own admission, Woerner had played poorly in Georgia's first two games of the season. Bell, on the other hand, had played well in a reserve role. Woerner had started every game since the 1978 season opener but had to surrender his starting left cornerback position for the Clemson contest.

Clemson sophomore quarterback Homer Jordan was returning home to square off against former high school teammates Amp Arnold and Jimmy Payne and the rest of the Georgia Bulldogs. An all-state player at Athens' Cedar Shoals High School, Jordan chose Clemson over Georgia when he was told he would play a position other than quarterback for the Bulldogs.

Scott Woerner streaks down the sideline after intercepting a Clemson pass in his own end zone. He was not tackled until reaching the Tigers' 2-yard line. *Photo courtesy of Wingate Downs.*

The strong-armed, quick-footed Jordan had seen limited playing time as a freshman for the Tigers, completing three of 11 passes for 28 yards in 1979. Nevertheless, Homer was named Clemson's starter in '80 and passed for 142 yards and rushed for another 68 in the Tigers' season-opening victory a week prior to facing the Bulldogs.

Late in the opening quarter, Georgia held a 7–0 advantage, but Jordan had driven the Tigers to the Bulldogs' 11-yard line. On third down

HOMER JORDAN

    In his homecoming return to Athens, Georgia, Homer Jordan spent much of the day on the sideline watching backup quarterback Mike Gasque. Jordan was ineffective against the Bulldogs, losing four yards on eight carries and throwing for just 50 yards on five of 11 passing, including Scott Woerner's interception. Jordan's performance nearly lost him his starting job to Gasque; however, Jordan would eventually start every game for the Tigers in 1980.

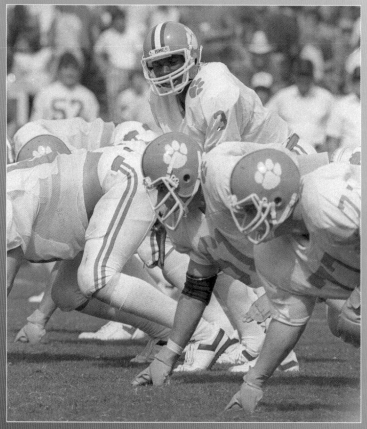

Clemson quarterback Homer Jordan did not fare well on his two return trips to his native Athens, losing in both 1980 and 1982. *Photo courtesy of Wingate Downs.*

As a junior in 1981, Jordan became a household name when he directed Clemson to a perfect 12-0 record and a national championship. In earning All-Atlantic Coast Conference honors, Jordan gained 2,116 yards of total offense, including 194 in a 13-3 upset win over Georgia. In 1982 Jordan threw four interceptions against the Bulldogs on his second return to Athens in a 13-7 Georgia victory. However, although he spent much of the season injured, Homer was instrumental in Clemson's 9-1-1 record and No. 8 national ranking. Jordan played four seasons from 1983 to 1986 in the Canadian Football League for three teams.

and nine, Jordan threw over the middle into the end zone. Woerner, who had recently entered the game, picked off the Athens native's pass a couple of yards behind his goal line. As he gained his footing in the end zone, Woerner noticed down the sideline that just one Tiger stood between him and the opposite goal line. "The Returner" Woerner, who had run a punt back for a touchdown earlier in the game, decided to return the interception out of his end zone.

Woerner headed to his right and began dashing down the sideline. The lone would-be tackler he had spotted between him and the goal line and been taken out of the play with a beautiful block by roverback Chris Welton. Woerner was not stopped until he had raced 98 yards and was caught from behind by tailback Chuck McSwain.

Herschel Walker rushed for one yard, and then Buck Belue followed with a one-yard sneak for a touchdown. Despite having run only five plays for minus-two yards in the first quarter, Georgia had jumped out to a 14–0 lead on two magnificent returns by Woerner. At halftime, the Bulldogs still led 14–10, despite the Tigers having a 16–0 advantage in first downs and a 25:10–4:50 upper hand in time of possession.

After rushing for only 12 yards in the first half, Walker gained 109 in the final two quarters, leading to two Georgia field goals. The Tigers kicked two field goals also and trailed 20–16 late in the game.

Clemson quarterback Mike Gasque, filling in for a benched Jordan, brought the Tigers to the Bulldogs' 10-yard line. On second and goal, with approximately two minutes remaining, Gasque's pass was tipped by linebacker Frank Ros and intercepted by safety Jeff Hipp to preserve Georgia's undefeated season.

On the first drive of the game, Clemson was forced to punt to Woerner, who returned the Tigers' kick 67 yards for a score. On Clemson's third

SCOTT WOERNER

Scott Woerner, considered Georgia's top college prospect out of high school, was a standout running back and defensive back at Jonesboro High School, coached by Weyman Sellers—cocaptain of Georgia's 1948 Southeastern Conference championship team.

While at Georgia, Woerner displayed a combination of skills at both defensive back and returning punts better than any Bulldog before him or since, other than perhaps Jake Scott. Woerner's 13 interceptions during his career tie him for fifth place in school history, his 839 kick return yards rank him seventh, and his 1,077 punt return yards were a Georgia record until 2003. Woerner was chosen first-team All-American in 1980.

Woerner is best remembered for his dazzling punt return for a touchdown against Georgia Tech in 1978; his two interceptions against Notre Dame in the '81 Sugar Bowl, when he was runner-up behind Herschel Walker in the MVP voting; and the two significant returns against Clemson in '80, without which the Bulldogs would have been defeated.

Woerner was an NFL third-round selection of Atlanta in 1981, leading the Falcons in punt returns as a rookie. He was a standout defensive back from 1983 to 1985 with the United States Football League's Philadelphia/Baltimore Stars, and he played for New Orleans in the NFL in 1987.

possession, the Tigers moved 49 yards to Georgia's 11-yard line. After a Clemson timeout following a Jordan incomplete pass on second down, the Tigers lined up in a flanked-left offensive formation opposite of the Bulldogs' man-to-man pass coverage. Woerner's responsibility was to cover the tight end, who, on the play, blocked for Jordan instead of running a pass route. Woerner responded by running into the passing lane, intercepting the pass, and ruining Homer's homecoming.

Game Details

Georgia 20 • Clemson 16

Date: September 20, 1980

Site: Sanford Stadium

Attendance: 60,800

Records: Georgia 2-0; Clemson 1-0

Rankings: Georgia: No. 10 (AP)/ No. 9 (UPI)

Series: Georgia 32-13-3 (Clemson one-game winning streak)

> What a day [Woerner] had.... He gave us the [first] 14 points of the game, really.
>
> **—Vince Dooley, Georgia head coach**

LEFT, RIGHT, LEFT, TOUCHDOWN

Charley Trippi zigzags through Tulsa for a startling 68-yard punt return

Halfback Charley Trippi had returned from military service during the 1945 season just in time to lead the Bulldogs to devastating defeats of Chattanooga, Florida, Auburn, and Georgia Tech by a combined 136–7 score. Georgia was rewarded with a trip to the first annual Oil Bowl in Houston against No. 17 Tulsa. Rumors had persisted leading up to the game that Charley Trippi possibly was going to sign a professional contract after the bowl game and bypass his senior year. With 27,000 in attendance, a near-sellout crowd at Rice Stadium, the game was considered a toss-up, with hopes for a Georgia victory being pinned on the performance of the great and perhaps departing Trippi.

In the final quarter, with Georgia leading 14–6, Tulsa was forced to punt. Hardy Brown punted to Trippi, who had averaged 20 yards on 11 punt returns during the regular season. From his own 32-yard line, Trippi ran diagonally from one sideline to the other, zigzagging as far back as

Blockers, including J.P. Miller (No. 53), clear a path for Charley Trippi (No. 62) as he returns a Tulsa punt 68 yards for a touchdown in the 1946 Oil Bowl. *Photo courtesy of AP Images.*

his own 20-yard line. Trying to pick up blocking, Trippi began heading back to the sideline where he first started his return. Finally, Georgia blockers began opening a running lane for Trippi. He first ran past some would-be tacklers, faked one Tulsa defender off balance, and then proceeded to head down the side. Trippi reached Tulsa's 10-yard line, where it appeared he would be tackled; two Golden Hurricane players were waiting to knock him out of bounds. Trippi lowered his head and attempted to run right through them. As the junior wonder rammed into the two Tulsa players, both crashed off Trippi's shoulders. Trippi continued on into the end zone for a heart-stirring, 68-yard touchdown.

CHARLEY TRIPPI

Charley Trippi, son of a coal miner from Pittston, Pennsylvania, wanted to attend Fordham University in New York City out of high school. That is where most of the kids from his area went to college. Harold "War Eagle" Ketron, captain of the Red and Black's 1903 squad, approached Trippi and recruited him to play at Georgia. Ketron lived in nearby Wilkes-Barre, Pennsylvania, and was the manager of a Coca-

Some still declare that Trippi's unbelievable return against Tulsa is the greatest punt return in the history of football. *Photo courtesy of AP Images.*

Cola plant. He promised Trippi that as long as he went to Georgia, he would have a job at his plant. As Trippi recalls, he graduated from high school on a Friday. The following Monday, he was driving a Coca-Cola truck for Ketron.

There was much more in store for Trippi than driving a truck in Wilkes-Barre. At Georgia, as he displayed in the '46 Oil Bowl, he was a star rusher, passer, receiver, punter, and returner—the entire package. According to author Loran Smith, Georgia quarterback John Rauch (1945-1948) compared Trippi to Michael Jordan. They are the only players Rauch saw in his life that could dominate a sport as they did.

In Georgia's first bowl game in three years, the Bulldogs scored first on a four-yard run by Charles "Rabbit" Smith. Georgia reached inside Tulsa's 18-yard line on two other occasions in the opening period but came away empty-handed.

Tulsa outplayed the Bulldogs in both the second and third quarters. Camp Wilson scored for the Golden Hurricane, pulling Tulsa within one point. Leading 7–6 in the fourth quarter, Trippi connected with John Donaldson for a 65-yard touchdown pass. On Tulsa's next possession, Brown punted to Trippi, and the result is still proclaimed by many as the greatest punt return in the history of football.

There are several reasons why Trippi's return was so spectacular. First, he ran from sideline to sideline, then returned to his original sideline, all the while losing ground as he waited for blocking to develop. In the process, he lost more than 10 yards from where he first began his return. Second, in reversing his field and zigzagging through Tulsa players, Trippi covered much more than 68 yards on the ground. Some onlookers estimated that he easily ran for at least twice the yardage he got credit for and might have covered as many as 200 yards in total. Lastly, after all the reversing and running, Trippi somehow had the strength to bowl over the two remaining would-be tacklers standing in his way of a touchdown.

Charles "Rabbit" Smith came to Georgia at a most opportune time. In 1943 Frank Sinkwich had graduated, and Charley Trippi had been summoned by the military. This resulted in playing opportunities for Smith and other 17-year-olds too young for the World War II draft.

As Sinkwich and Trippi had in '42, Smith and teammate Johnny Cook starred in Georgia's backfield on its war-torn teams of 1943 and 1944. Smith was small but quick, weighing approximately 155 pounds. Against Kentucky in 1945, the game prior to Trippi's return to the team, Rabbit rushed for 212 yards—the first official 200-yard rushing performance in Georgia football history. As Trippi led the Bulldogs' ground attack in the last half of the 1945 and 1946 seasons, Smith was relegated to second-string status. Nevertheless, he finished his collegiate career with 133 career points, including 22 touchdowns scored and an extra-point conversion.

Coach Wally Butts (seated at center) surrounds himself with members of his nine-win Oil Bowl champions of 1945. Included are Trippi (standing, second from right), Charles "Rabbit" Smith (seated, right), and John Rauch (standing, third from left).
Photo courtesy of AP Images.

Like Trippi, Smith played for the 1947 NFL champions Chicago Cardinals. While his teammate led the Cardinals in receiving and kick returns and was second in rushing, Smith played a minor role, rushing for 23 yards and intercepting a pass in seven games. Too small to play professional football, Smith's NFL career lasted just one season, and he would eventually enter coaching.

After his awe-inspiring performance in the 20–6 win over Tulsa, Trippi, for the sake of the Georgia football program and its faithful following, dispelled the rumor of him turning professional early. Reportedly, the Bulldogs had entered the Oil Bowl counting on Trippi's rushing, passing, and punting to lead them to victory. From the all-everything back, Georgia got in return the aforementioned, plus a brilliant, 68-yard exhibition into the end zone and a promise to return for the 1946 season.

Game Details

Georgia 20 • Tulsa 6

Date: January 1, 1946

Site: Oil Bowl

Attendance: 27,000

Records: Georgia 8–2; Tulsa 8–2

Rankings: Georgia: No. 18 (AP); Tulsa: No. 17 (AP)

Series: First meeting

> I started to the left then went to the right then back to the left and picked up my blocking.
>
> **—Charley Trippi, halfback**

BUTLER'S BOOMING GAME-WINNER

With only seconds remaining, Kevin Butler stuns second-ranked Clemson with a 60-yard, game-winning field goal

During the late 1970s and for most of the '80s, perhaps there was no bigger and more hated rival for the Bulldogs—including Florida, Auburn, and Georgia Tech—than the Clemson Tigers. Georgia and Clemson had begun the decade of the 1980s by each winning a national championship. Entering the 1984 encounter, both teams had won three games and played to a tie in their previous seven meetings. The Bulldogs were tackling no paper tiger in '84; Clemson was ranked No. 2 in the Associated Press Poll and was considered likely the best Tigers team ever at the school, including the 1981 national title squad. Despite having won 25 of its previous 26 games at Sanford Stadium, Georgia, a three-and-a-half-point underdog, was not favored at home for the first time since hosting Louisiana State in 1979.

Kevin Butler (center) trots off the field with lineman Mike Weaver (No. 63) after making his 60-yard winning field goal against Clemson in 1984. Butler's kick broke a 23–23 tie with 11 seconds remaining and tied an SEC record for the longest field goal. *Photo courtesy of Wingate Downs.*

The underdog Bulldogs had rallied and were tied with the Tigers, 23–23, in the final quarter. Georgia faced fourth down from Clemson's 44-yard line with 17 seconds remaining. The Bulldogs had only one option: Coach Vince Dooley raised his hand in the air and ordered, "Field goal!" The field goal attempt would be from more than 60 yards. Although none longer had been made in the history of the Southeastern Conference, Dooley had confidence in his place-kicker, Kevin Butler, who had kicked a 70-yarder earlier that week in practice.

From Georgia's own 49½-yard line, Butler took his accustomed three steps back and two steps to the side from the kicking tee. Holder Jimmy Harrell took the snap, and Butler boomed a perfect 60-yard kick through the uprights as Sanford Stadium became absolutely unhinged.

Actually, the senior place-kicker's field goal would have been good from 65 yards out and perhaps even 70.

With 11 seconds left to play, Clemson's Ray Williams caught Butler's ensuing kickoff on his own 20-yard line and ran 10 yards. Suddenly, Williams threw the ball across the field to teammate Terrance Roulhac, who began streaking down his left sideline. He ran out of bounds at Georgia's 35-yard line, hoping to set up a game-tying field goal by

TODD WILLIAMS

Todd Williams' father, Dale, was a reserve quarterback at Georgia from 1959 to 1961. In 1981, Todd was chosen State Back of the Year, guiding Waycross High School to Georgia's AAA state championship coached by his father. Todd backed up John Lastinger at quarterback in 1982 and 1983. After rallying the Bulldogs to tie Clemson in '83, Williams was giving the starting nod over Lastinger the following week against South Carolina before being injured in the third quarter.

As a junior in 1984, Williams directed an inexperienced Bulldogs offense; only two starters returned from the year prior. After an outstanding performance in the season opener against Southern Mississippi, when he completed 12 of 16 passes for 123 yards, with no interceptions, and rushed for 38 yards, Williams was dreadful versus Clemson before reviving the Bulldogs' young offense in the second half. The five interceptions he threw against the Tigers, four in the first half alone, were as many as he had his entire senior year in high school. Williams later said he was praying just prior to Kevin Butler's game-winning field-goal attempt against Clemson, hoping the place-kicker would get the quarterback "off the hook."

Hampered by injuries, Williams missed three regular-season games during his junior campaign, most of the '84 Citrus Bowl, and was redshirted in 1985. Williams returned in 1986 as a backup to James Jackson and Wayne Johnson, attempting just one pass the entire season.

Clemson's accomplished kicker, Donald Igwebuike. Fortunately for Georgia, it was ruled that Roulhac went out of bounds with no time remaining. The game was over, and the Bulldogs had won 26–23 against their bitter rival.

Taking advantage of four interceptions thrown by Georgia's Todd Williams in the first half, the Tigers held a comfortable 20–6 halftime advantage. Perhaps catching an overconfident Clemson squad off guard,

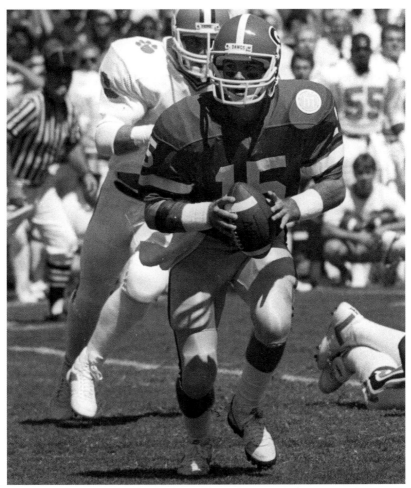

Quarterback Todd Williams struggled in the first half against the Tigers, completing just three of 11 passes and throwing four interceptions. However, in the second half he rallied the Bulldogs to an eventual upset victory over the No. 2-ranked team in the country. *Photo courtesy of Wingate Downs.*

the Bulldogs finally began to generate some offense in the third quarter. Georgia scored a touchdown on a pass from Williams to Herman Archie, and later in the quarter, key completions by Williams to Andre "Pulpwood" Smith and Archie led to a one-yard touchdown run by Cleveland Gary. A fourth-quarter field goal by Butler gave Georgia a short-lived lead as an Igwebuike field goal tied the game 23–23 late in the contest.

The Bulldogs began their final possession on their 20-yard line with 2:10 remaining on the clock. Two consecutive short completions from Williams to Fred Lane and Tron Jackson earned a first down to the 31-yard line. After an incomplete pass, Jackson ripped off a 24-yard gain to Clemson's 45. With 1:19 left, Williams completed a pass for only one yard and followed with back-to-back incompletions, setting up fourth and nine at the 44-yard line.

Game Details

Georgia 26 • Clemson 23

Date: September 22, 1984

Site: Sanford Stadium

Attendance: 82,122

Records: Georgia 1–0; Clemson 2–0

Rankings: Georgia: No. 20 (AP)/ No. 17 (UPI); Clemson: No. 2 (AP)/ Not ranked by UPI because of probation

Series: Georgia 34–14–4 (16–16 tie in 1983)

> It was one of the sweetest kicks I've had. It's the best feeling I've ever had.
>
> **—Kevin Butler, place-kicker**

Butler had shockingly missed a 26-yard field goal earlier in the game, his first failed kick of fewer than 30 yards since his freshman campaign. However, he had already made seven field goals in less than two games for the season. In addition, he was aided with a 10-mile-per-hour wind at his back.

As he jogged onto the field to attempt his game-winning try, Butler recalled that no one said a word to him except his holder, Harrell, who told him only to keep his head down and kick the ball hard. Butler obliged, knocking through the longest and maybe the most celebrated field goal in conference history.

KEVIN BUTLER

Following Georgia's 1980 national championship season, one of the biggest concerns of Coach Vince Dooley was replacing two-time All-American place-kicker Rex Robinson. As it would turn out, Kevin Butler was more than sufficient in succeeding Robinson and became arguably the greatest kicker in the history of college football.

Butler rewrote Georgia and the Southeastern Conference's record book for kicking. He finished in the top 10 nationally each of his four seasons in successful field goals per game, and upon graduation, his 77 career field goals ranked second in the history of college football. Butler was a four-time All-SEC performer and was chosen first-team All-American in 1983 and 1984, including consensus All-American as a senior. Of the more than 900 players in the College Football Hall of Fame as of 2015, Butler, inducted in 2001, is the sole place-kicker.

In 13 seasons (1985–1997) in the NFL, Butler kicked 265 field goals and scored 1,208 points with Chicago and Arizona. He is still close to Georgia's football program, and his son Drew was a punter on the Bulldogs squad from 2008 to 2011.

HEARTBREAKERS

THE TIMEOUT

Disputed timeout called by Florida negates Georgia's potential game-winning score

The Bulldogs at 1–4 were absolutely dreadful during the first half of the 1993 campaign, losing twice as many games as they had lost the entire season before. However, behind one of the best quarterbacks in the nation, junior Eric Zeier, and a set of gifted receivers, "Air Georgia" finally reached its full potential and won three consecutive games by the end of October.

Next on the schedule was Steve Spurrier's Florida Gators and their feared offense, the "Fun 'n' Gun." The Gators were an overwhelming favorite to defeat Georgia with an offense averaging an eye-popping 40 points and 514 yards per game for the season. In three consecutive wins over the Bulldogs, the "Fun 'n' Gun" averaged more than 36 points per contest while defeating Georgia by more than three touchdowns per victory. It certainly appeared the '93 Georgia senior class would be the first to lose four straight to Florida in 30 years (1960–1963).

To the astonishment of practically everyone, the Bulldogs trailed by only one touchdown late

Against Florida in 1993, Eric Zeier's touchdown pass to Jerry Jerman with only seconds remaining was negated by the officials. *Photo courtesy of Wingate Downs.*

in the game. In the final seconds, Zeier completed a 12-yard touchdown pass to Jerry Jerman to pull Georgia within a point, 33–32. Just as a game-winning two-point conversion for Georgia was envisioned, the Bulldogs faithful received some disappointing news. Supposedly, Florida cornerback Anthone Lott called timeout just before Zeier took the snap on the negated scoring pass. The play was called dead with five seconds left in the game, and Georgia still trailed by seven points instead of one. The Bulldogs had two shots at the end zone but could not score and lost to the Gators once again.

The day was as dreary as the first five games of Georgia's season, as swirling winds and a steady rain drenched the Gator Bowl. Down

ERIC ZEIER

When the action was not nearly as commonplace as it is today, Eric Zeier enrolled early at Georgia out of high school and participated in spring drills prior to his freshman season of 1991. He was regarded as one of the better quarterbacks in the SEC as a freshman and sophomore. In 1993 the Bulldogs were without running back Garrison Hearst and an adequate running game and were forced to throw the ball more often. Over his final two seasons, Zeier eclipsed most school and many conference passing and total offense records.

Zeier is regarded by many as the greatest quarterback ever at Georgia. Since Zeke Bratkowski in the early 1950s, Zeier is the only Bulldogs signal caller chosen first-team All-American (1994). Besides Ray Goff (1976), Zeier is the lone Georgia quarterback to finish in the Heisman Trophy's top 10 voting, and he did it twice (10th in 1993, seventh in 1994).

Since playing in the NFL from 1995 to 2000, Zeier has enjoyed a successful business career. In addition, at the start of the 2007 season, he was selected as Georgia's new color analyst on its radio broadcast team.

13–3 in the first quarter, the Bulldogs rallied to take a 20–13 lead in the second quarter. "Air Georgia" was in full effect as Zeier would attempt a whopping 65 passes for the game, one shy of an SEC record, while the Bulldogs would attempt only 14 rushes in the entire contest. Of Zeier's 36 completions, tight end Shannon Mitchell caught 15—a school record that still stands today.

Spurrier benched quarterback and freshman phenom Danny Wuerffel and abandoned the pass; the 21 pass attempts were a low for Florida since Spurrier's arrival. The "Fun 'n' Gun" turned to the running game and Errict Rhett, who finished with 183 rushing yards on a school-record 41 carries.

Florida regained the lead, 23–20, before halftime and held a 10-point advantage late in the game. Nonetheless, Georgia's Kanon Parkman kicked his fourth field goal with 5:06 remaining, and the Bulldogs

Game Details

Florida 33 • Georgia 26

Date: October 30, 1993

Site: Gator Bowl

Attendance: 80,392

Records: Georgia 4–4; Florida 5–1

Rankings: Florida: No. 10 (AP)/ No. 10 (CNN)

Series: Georgia 44–25–2 (Florida three-game winning streak)

> The game was stolen from us, stolen by the refs.
>
> **—Mitch Davis, Georgia linebacker**

trailed only 33–26. Georgia would get the ball back on its own 36-yard line with just 1:36 left on the clock and time for one last possession.

The Bulldogs reached Florida's 12-yard line with only seconds remaining. Just as the ball was snapped, Lott noticed the Gators sideline was screaming for a timeout because Florida had only 10 players on the field. Lott asked a nearby judge for the timeout, and Georgia's potential winning play was waved off by the official.

Pass interference on Florida was the call on an incomplete Zeier pass, and the Bulldogs advanced to the Gators' 2-yard line with no time

STEVE SPURRIER

Known as the "Ol' Ball Coach" and the "Evil Genius," Steve Spurrier seemingly has had a longtime disdain for Georgia football, and vice versa. As Florida's quarterback, he faced the Bulldogs three times (1964–1966), defeating Georgia in '65 on a touchdown pass in the final minutes.

As the first-year head coach at Florida in 1990, Spurrier's Gators were leading the Dogs 38–7 toward the end of the game. Georgia's reserve offense was on the field and close to making one of the team's few first downs for the game. Spurrier's reaction was to take out his reserve defensive unit and insert the first team during the blowout. In subsequent years, Spurrier often made snide and ridiculing remarks about Georgia football, occasionally during postgame interviews when Florida had soundly defeated the Bulldogs.

Even Spurrier's own players have admitted in the past that their coach did not think too much of Georgia. As one story goes, the dislike stems from a 27–10 Bulldogs victory over Florida in Spurrier's Heisman Trophy–winning campaign of 1966. Spurrier won just one of three games against Georgia as Florida's quarterback.

on the clock and were granted one final play. Zeier threw behind and incomplete to Jeff Thomas, and Florida escaped with a 33–26 victory.

While the Gators rejoiced, several Georgia players were dazed, staggering, and crying uncontrollably, still disbelieving their earlier touchdown had been waved off and six points had been taken off the scoreboard.

Florida quarterback Steve Spurrier confers with his coach, Ray Graves, in 1967. Although Spurrier was extremely successful as the Gators' head coach against Georgia, he only defeated the Bulldogs once as a player. *Photo courtesy of AP Images.*

Television replays clearly proved that Zeier had taken the snap and was dropping back with the ball prior to the official calling the touchdown play dead. However, the rules state that as soon as an official *sees* a player call timeout, as soon as he "receives it in his mind," the play is dead.

The setback was one of many disappointing defeats for Georgia in what was a Gators-dominated series during the 1990s. Unfortunately, a chance at victory was taken away from the Bulldogs in '93, a possible victory over Florida that was hard to come by for an entire decade.

During the regular-season finale of 1993, his junior season, quarterback Eric Zeier passes for some of his 328 yards in a 43-10 victory over Georgia Tech. Sixteen days later he finished 10th in the Heisman Trophy voting, and he finished seventh the following year. To date, Zeier is only one of three Bulldogs, along with Frank Sinkwich and Herschel Walker, to finish in the Heisman's top-ten voting in two or more seasons. *Photo courtesy of AP Images.*

JASPER SANKS' PHANTOM FUMBLE

An erroneous ruling arises as Georgia drives for winning score against Tech in '99

Georgia and Georgia Tech entered their gridiron contest in 1999 with identical but somewhat disappointing 7–3 records. Led by high-powered offenses, both teams had lofty expectations only to have their defenses falter in upset losses. The Bulldogs sought revenge as the Yellow Jackets had won the previous year, following a controversial call on a fumble. Georgia had held a 19–7 fourth-quarter lead, but Georgia Tech, behind quarterback Joe Hamilton, cut its deficit to a single point. On the game's winning drive, Hamilton fumbled, and the Bulldogs recovered the ball. However, officials called it otherwise, and Georgia Tech maintained possession. Soon afterward, Tech's Brad Chambers kicked a 35-yard field goal with two seconds remaining, snapping Tech's seven-game losing streak to Georgia. A year later, the

In 1999 Georgia Tech fans and players celebrate after handing Georgia a 51–48 overtime defeat, likely the Bulldogs' most heartbreaking loss in years. *Photo courtesy of Georgia Tech Athletic Association.*

JASPER SANKS

Perhaps the most-hyped Georgia football recruit since Herschel Walker besides Matthew Stafford was running back Jasper Sanks. Sanks was a *USA Today* and *Parade* magazine first-team All-American at Carver-Columbus High School. When he signed with Georgia prior to the 1997 season, the Bulldogs faithful instantly envisioned him as the school's next great back. However, Sanks' career is generally recognized more as five years of disappointment than anything else.

Sanks' lackluster football career at Georgia began with his failing to make the qualifying entrance exam scores. After a year at Fork Union Military Academy, Sanks carried the ball only 10 times as a freshman in '98. As a sophomore, he led the Bulldogs with nearly 900 yards rushing but lost two critical fumbles that season: one versus Florida, which ended momentum Georgia had gained in the game, and the other the aforementioned "nonfumble" against Georgia Tech. Sanks'

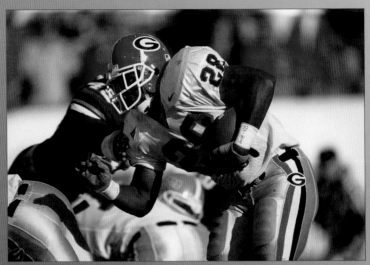

Although he had a respectable playing career at Georgia, Jasper Sanks was unfortunately better known for his off-the-field troubles and his two prominent lost fumbles in 1999—the first coming against Florida followed by the "phantom" fumble at Georgia Tech. *Photo courtesy of Getty Images.*

final two seasons were characterized by fluctuating weight, diminished quickness, and injuries as he combined for only 690 rushing yards in 2000 and 2001. Against Auburn in 2001, Sanks was stopped short of the goal line on Georgia's final play in a seven-point loss. By the end of the year, he was dismissed from the team for rules violations, and with that, his football career came to an end.

Jasper Sanks' playing days at Georgia were not a complete disappointment. His three consecutive 130-yard rushing performances toward the beginning of his sophomore season have been achieved by few at the school. Sanks' 1,651 career rushing yards rank 20th in school history, ahead of such notables as Keith Henderson, Ronnie Jenkins, Horace King, and Theron Sapp. Most admirably, the 21-year-old showed courage after his fumble and Georgia's loss to Georgia Tech in 1999. While some prominent teammates refused to answer questions after the defeat, namely a dejected Quincy Carter, Sanks bravely stood tall and faced the media. Among his comments, the young running back said it was a "bizarre" game and echoed what everyone else witnessed that day—he was undoubtedly down on the ground when the football popped out of his grasp.

Dogs would experience déjà vu, losing a fumble on a questionable call and then losing the game on a field goal.

In a tied 48–48 contest, Georgia had a first down and goal on Georgia Tech's 2-yard line with 13 seconds remaining. Instead of attempting a field goal, Bulldogs coach Jim Donnan elected to run one more play. Sophomore Jasper Sanks ran a dive at left guard, falling just short of the 1-yard line. After being tackled and clearly down, Sanks lost the football. Tech safety Chris Young, hoping the ball was still in play, picked up the apparently dead ball just outside the end zone, ran behind his goal line, and curiously ran to the sideline to hand the ball to coach George O'Leary. As Georgia ran its field-goal unit onto the field, Georgia Tech was awarded possession by the officials.

Georgia was forced to play in overtime. In the extra period's first drive, quarterback Quincy Carter threw an interception. From Georgia's

25-yard line, Georgia Tech ran two plays for four yards and elected to kick a field goal on third down. Luke Manget's kick was blocked by Kendrell Bell. Nonetheless, holder George Godsey recovered the block behind the line of scrimmage, ran for five yards, and the Yellow Jackets had regained possession on Georgia's 21-yard line. After he had headed off the field, dejected because his kick was blocked, Manget was given another chance at victory on fourth down. His second 38-yard attempt was successful, and Georgia Tech prevailed in overtime, 51–48.

As they had done for most of the season, both squads displayed exceptional offenses but exhibited subpar defenses. The teams combined for 1,102 total yards and nearly 100 points. Hamilton threw for 341 yards and four touchdowns and led all rushers with 94 yards

Game Details

Georgia Tech 51 • Georgia 48

Date: November 27, 1999

Site: Bobby Dodd Stadium

Attendance: 46,450

Records: Georgia 7–3; Georgia Tech 7–3

Rankings: Georgia: No. 16 (AP)/ No. 21 (ESPN); Georgia Tech: No. 20 (AP)/ No. 16 (ESPN)

Series: Georgia 52–34–5 (Georgia Tech one-game winning streak)

> It looks like [the game's officials] had a miss.... It certainly appears...that [Sanks] was down.
>
> **—Bobby Gaston, the SEC's supervisor of football officials**

on 15 carries. Carter passed for 345 yards on 29 of 55 passing and was responsible for three touchdowns.

Georgia trailed by 17 points on two occasions in the third quarter, including once with only 17 minutes to play in the game. The Bulldogs scored 24 consecutive points and led 48–41, but Georgia Tech rallied and tied the contest with 2:37 remaining. In the final minutes, Georgia drove 62 yards in nine plays. Sanks carried twice for 25 yards to reach the Yellow Jackets' 2-yard line.

On Jasper Sanks' "nonfumble," side judge Ron Leatherwood correctly signaled Georgia's ball; however, he was overruled by umpire Bud Williams. Three of the four officials initially said there was no fumble, although head referee Al Ford would later comment that two of his officials saw the ball pop out before the play was dead. They were incorrect in their assessment, as television replays undeniably showed that Sanks was down prior to fumbling the football.

The game's officials, regarded as the best in the Southeastern Conference, were scheduled to officiate the following week's SEC Championship Game until their blunder; they were suspended by the conference for their mistake. Several seasons later, instant replay was established in college football to prohibit similar errors from occurring. This action by the NCAA came just a few years too late for Georgia's "phantom fumble" of 1999.

A FIRST IN FOOTBALL

Albeit illegal and a fluke, Georgia allows football's first forward pass in 1895

When Georgia and North Carolina faced one another for the first time in 1895, both teams were considered the schools' best ever in their short histories of playing football. The Red and Black's starting 11 averaged 167 pounds per man, interestingly considered heavy at the time. Even more intriguing was the fact that George Butler was playing for the Tar Heels. Butler was a standout quarterback and extra-point specialist on Georgia's first three teams (1892–1894) and was captain of the '93 and '94 squads.

Nevertheless, the game would become even more compelling and noteworthy shortly after its start. What was intended as a punt turned into a George Stephens–to–Joel Whitaker touchdown toss for a North Carolina touchdown—football's first forward pass.

Prior to the forward pass being allowed by the game's rules, football was more like a rugby scrum than the sport we know of today. During the first few minutes of the Georgia–North Carolina contest, the rugby style of play, as usual, was on display in a scoreless tie.

Although they finished with a losing 3–4 record, the 1895 Red and Black were considered one of the better teams in the South. Nevertheless, they may be most remembered as the team that yielded football's very first forward pass. *Photo courtesy of Hargrett Rare Book & Manuscript Library/University of Georgia Libraries.*

According to author John Stegeman, some of the spectators at Athletic Park, including Auburn head coach John Heisman, scouting for his game against Georgia a month later, were unwilling to remain on the sidelines. Instead, they situated themselves on the field behind the offensive team. Georgia fumbled on the game's first possession, and four minutes into the contest, North Carolina was forced to punt after a series of short gains. Stephens retreated to kick "only to find himself trapped between the oncharging Georgia linemen and the fans who had lined up behind the Carolina team. Coach Heisman, for one, had to duck to keep out of the way."

Instead of punting, Stephens threw a desperation forward pass downfield to teammate Whitaker. Whitaker caught the ball, ran through

GLENN "POP" WARNER

After playing collegiate football at Cornell University and graduating from its law school, Glenn "Pop" Warner began his illustrious football coaching career at the University of Georgia at the young age of 24. He signed a 10-week contract to coach the Red and Black's 1895 squad for $34 per week.

Upon witnessing Georgia's pathetic athletic field for the first time and having only 12 players around which to build his team, Warner longed for Cornell and northeastern football. However, he quickly got over his reservations. Although Georgia finished with a losing 3-4 record in 1895, the Red and Black were considered one of the best teams in the South. Warner's 1896 team recorded a perfect 4-0 mark—one of only three undefeated and untied seasons in Georgia football history.

Warner left Georgia to coach his alma mater in 1897. For 44 uninterrupted seasons, the "Gridiron's Greatest Strategist" coached six institutions to a remarkable 319-106-32 career record.

After coaching at Georgia for only two years, Glenn "Pop" Warner went on to coach five other schools for 42 additional seasons. He is still regarded as one of college football's greatest coaches. *Photo courtesy of AP Images.*

Red and Black defenders like "lightning," and crossed Georgia's goal line. The referee signaled a North Carolina touchdown, claiming he had not seen the illegal pass. The Red and Black faithful were incensed. A fight between players on the opposing teams might have led to a riot if not for the presence of Atlanta Chief of Police Arthur B. Connolly and his patrolmen.

Besides the fortuitous fluke, neither side scored the rest of the game, and North Carolina held on to the 6–0 victory. The next day, newspapers hardly knew how to describe football's first forward pass. *The Atlanta Journal* portrayed the play as a "fumble[d] pass" in addition to a "bad pass."

Although Georgia was on the opposing side of the successful illegal pass, the school had an impact on the play's eventual acceptance as a facet of football's offensive arsenal. In 1905, Heisman wrote to Walter

Game Details

North Carolina 6 • Georgia 0

Date: October 26, 1895

Site: Athletic Park

Attendance: 1,000

Records: Georgia 1–0; North Carolina 2–0

Series: First meeting

> This was clearly a fluke, but then [fluke plays] count for just as much as hard-earned plays.
>
> *—Atlanta Constitution*

Camp, head of a collegiate football rules committee and "Father of American Football," describing the forward pass he witnessed in Atlanta 10 years prior and recommending that it become a part of the sport's rules "in order to open up the game."

A year later, on September 5, 1906, St. Louis University's Bradbury Robinson threw football's first legal pass incomplete against Carroll College of Wisconsin. However, on his next attempt, Robinson completed a 20-yard pass to teammate Jack Schneider for a touchdown.

JOHN HEISMAN

Coach John Heisman must have scouted Georgia well in its game against North Carolina in 1895, as his first Auburn team defeated the Red and Black 16-6 later that season.

Prior to five seasons at Auburn, Heisman coached at Oberlin College and the University of Akron for three combined years. From 1900 to 1927, he had successful stints at Clemson, Georgia Tech, University of Pennsylvania, Washington and Jefferson College, and Rice University, and captured a national title at Georgia Tech in 1917. He remains tied for first in NCAA history for most schools as a head coach with eight and finished with an accomplished 185-70-17 record. Other accomplishments include the Heisman Trophy, annually given to college football's most outstanding player, being named in his honor.

Heisman is also characterized as an innovator of football, including bringing the forward pass to the game after first witnessing Georgia allow North Carolina's "fluke" play in 1895.

SOURCES

Athens Banner-Herald (1895–2014).

Atlanta Constitution (1895–2014).

Atlanta Journal (1910–2014).

Augusta Chronicle (1913–2014).

Birmingham News (November 21, 1920).

Bolton, Clyde. *Silver Britches: Inside University of Georgia Football.* West Point, NY: Leisure Press, 1982.

Cromartie, Bill. *Clean Old-Fashioned Hate.* Nashville: Rutledge Hill Press, 1987.

Garbin, Patrick. *About Them Dawgs!: Georgia Football's Memorable Teams and Players.* Lanham, MD: The Scarecrow Press, Inc., 2008.

———. *"Then Vince Said to Herschel...": The Best Georgia Bulldog Stories Ever Told.* Chicago: Triumph Books, 2007.

Martin, Charles E. *I've Seen 'Em All.* Athens, GA: The McGregor Company, 1961.

National Collegiate Athletic Association. *Official 2007 NCAA Divisions I Football Records Book.* Indianapolis: The National Collegiate Athletic Association, 2007.

Red and Black [independent University of Georgia newspaper] 1913–1976.

Rivalries: The Tradition of Georgia vs. Florida. DVD. New York: Hart Sharp Video, 2003.

Seiler, Sonny, and Kent Hannon. *Damn Good Dogs!: The Real Story of Uga, the University of Georgia's Bulldog Mascots.* Athens, GA: Hill Street Press, 2002.

Sewanee: The University of the South. *Football Media Guide*. 2007.

Stegeman, John F. *The Ghosts of Herty Field: Early Days on a Southern Gridiron*. Athens, GA: University of Georgia Press, 1997.

Thilenius, Ed, and Jim Koger. *No Ifs, No Ands, a Lot of Butts: 21 Years of Georgia Football*. Atlanta: Foote and Davies, Inc., 1960.

University of Georgia. *Football Media Guide*, 1948–2014.

Woodruff, Fuzzy. *A History of Southern Football (1890–1928)*. Vol. 1. Atlanta: Walter W. Brown Publishing Co., 1928.